STEP BY STEP
WITH ON1 PHOTO
RAW

START-TO-FINISH TUTORIALS FOR THE CREATIVE PHOTOGRAPHER

NICOLE S. YOUNG

STEP BY STEP WITH ON1 PHOTO RAW

Start-to-Finish Tutorials for the Creative Photographer

Nicole S. Young

Published by Nicolesy®, Inc.
www.nicolesy.com

Copy editor: Linda Laflamme
Indexer: Valerie Haynes Perry
Layout, Design, and Photography: Nicole S. Young
Author Photo: © dav.d

NOTICE OF RIGHTS

LIABILITY

TRADEMARKS

ISBN-13: 978-0-9982613-3-1
ISBN-10: 0-9982613-3-5

www.nicolesy.com

I N T R O D U C T I O N

ON1 Photo is a powerful program that is created for photographers, allowing artists to stylize and polish their photographs with ease. I've been using this program for years as a complement to my workflow within Adobe® Lightroom® and Photoshop®, and with the newest update the program has become even more powerful. ON1 Photo RAW now allows photographers to edit Raw images using the brand new Develop module, adding the capability of a complete start-to-finish workflow entirely within ON1 Photo.

In this book, I will take you through several photographs from beginning to end, all edited inside of ON1 Photo RAW. To give you a little more insight into what you can expect, below is a quick Q&A on this book and the new ON1 Photo RAW software.

WHAT'S NEW IN ON1 PHOTO RAW?

The newest version of ON1 Photo brings with it the ability to nondestructively edit Raw photographs. This very big update to their software now makes it possible to edit a photo from start to finish entirely inside of ON1 Photo.

Some of the major updates include a new Develop module that allows you to nondestructively process Raw photographs (and replaces the Enhance module of previous versions), the merging of the Portrait module with Effects, and global presets (along with the ability to add a preset in either Browse, Develop, or Effects).

WHAT WILL I LEARN IN THIS BOOK?

This book shows practical and real-life start-to-finish examples of processing images using ON1 Photo RAW. By following along you will learn not only how to properly adjust white balance, tone, and other basic settings, but also go beyond the everyday adjustments by using layer masking to swap out skies, create beautiful double-exposures, stylize a photograph to make it look like an antique, and even add special effects to an image, such as fog and fireworks. You will also see inside of my workflow process and learn some of the best ways to edit a photograph from beginning to end.

DO I NEED TO USE RAW PHOTOS?

No! ON1 Photo RAW allows you to process Raw, JPEG, PSD, TIFF, and PNG files in every one of its modules. The Develop module is made specifically with Raw photographs in mind; however, you can still benefit from this software with other file types.

The advantage to using Raw files is that you have much more data to work with in the photograh and can create a cleaner edit when editing from start to finish in ON1 Photo. Adjustments, such as white balance and exposure, can be adjusted without severely degrading the quality of the image. I photograph all of my images in the Raw format and suggest that serious photographers do the same.

CAN I USE A DIFFERENT RAW EDITOR INSTEAD OF ON1?

Yes! ON1 Photo does not require that you edit your Raw photographs within the software. In fact, in my daily workflow I prefer to use Lightroom, and then I push my edited Raw photos into ON1 Photo for further processing and stylization.

DIGITAL DOWNLOADS

PRACTICE IMAGES

The tutorials in this book include free practice files that you can use to follow along with the step-by-step instructions throughout this book. Please use the link below to access this free download:

http://nicolesyblog.com/sbs-raw

EBOOK & VIDEO TUTORIALS

This book also comes in eBook and video format (sold separately), containing bonus video training where you can watch seven additional start-to-finish post-processing in action. Please use the link below for more information on these digital products:

https://store.nicolesy.com/products/step-by-step-raw

CHAPTER ONE

THE ON1 PHOTO RAW WORKSPACE

Before I dive into post-processing, I would first like to introduce you to the workspace you will be using to edit your photographs, as well as provide some advice regarding setting the general ON1 Photo preferences. This chapter is meant as a quick guide that describes many of the most important sections and tools, as well as lays everything out in an easy-to-read reference. Feel free to flip back to this chapter if you need a reminder on a tool or section as you make your way throughout the processing steps in this book.

BROWSE

The *Browse* module is the "home base" inside of ON1 Photo RAW, particularly if you plan on using it as your primary application to store and access your files. It makes jumping back and forth between photos and modules a breeze. It's also the preferred module to export your photographs (more on that in *Chapter 5*).

INDEXED FOLDERS

If you plan on using ON1 Photo as your main Raw processing software, then you will first want to *index* the folders where your images reside on your hard drive. If you have a top-level folder where all of your photos are located, then you may want to begin by adding that folder. To index a folder, click the **+** icon at the top of the panel and navigate to your main photos folder. Keep in mind that if you have a large collection of photographs, then it may take some time for the folder to fully index.

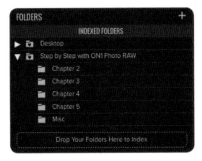

ORGANIZE WITH ALBUMS & SMART ALBUMS

The *Albums* panel is an efficient way to organize your photographs without moving them out of their existing folders. This section allows you to "collect" photographs from more than one folder and organize them together. For instance, you could group together photos to use in a photo album, your favorite landscape images, photos of your dog, and so on.

Smart Albums allow you to organize your photographs based on an attribute, metadata, or keywords. For example, if I create a Smart Album to store only the photographs that I have "liked," ON1 Photo RAW will automatically search my photographs and add them to the album.

SEARCH IMAGES THROUGH FILTERING

It is sometimes necessary to search through your photos, and that's where the *Filters* panel is helpful. Here you can search images based on their attributes (likes, dislikes, color label), when they were photographed, and also through keywords.

READ AND MODIFY THE METADATA

On the right side of the Browse module you can view the *metadata* for your file. Here you can edit the author name, description, and also the keywords for your images. There is also a panel that displays the EXIF and IPTC data, which will give you even more information about your image (exposure, date, camera, lens, and so on).

METADATA

Author Nicole S. Young
Description Plates of bruschetta.

Add Keyword
Keywords food, nicolesy, bruschetta, fujifilm

Show EXIF IPTC None

File Name bruschetta_0839.raf
Dimensions 6000x4000 @ 72 ppi
Capture Date Sep 20, 2016 • 9:07:41 AM
User Comment
GPS
Exposure 1/4 sec @ f/6.4
ISO 200
Exposure Bias
Focal Length 21 mm
Model X-T2
Lens FUJIFILM XF18-55mmF2.8-4 R LM OIS
Exposure Prog Shutter Priority AE
Flash Mode
Metering Mode Average
White Balance

THE BROWSE WORKSPACE (LEFT SIDE)

A   **Browse & Presets panel:** Accesses and applies saved Develop and Effects presets

B   **Breadcrumbs:** Displays the path of the selected folder or image

C   **Folders panel:** Displays folders by type: Indexed, Local Drives, or Cloud Storage

D   **Albums panel:** Organizes photos manually or automatically

E   **Shortcuts palette:** Allows quick access to some common photo storage locations

F   **Filters panel:** Searches your photos based on their attributes and keywords

G   **Recent panel:** Displays your most recently modified photographs

H   **Preferences icon:** Click to access the Preferences window

I   **Help Icon:** Click to bring up the ON1 support website (Internet required)

J   **Toggle left section (open/close):** Click to hide or reveal the left sidebar section

K   **Grid view:** Displays photos in a grid view (shown here)

L   **Detail view:** Displays a full-screen photo in the preview area

M   **Filmstrip:** Brings up a filmstrip view of your photos at the bottom of the window

N   **Thumbnail size:** Increases and decreases the size of the thumbnail

O   **Sort:** Displays the folder's sort order

P   **Star ratings:** Enables you to rate images on a scale of 1 star to 5 stars

Q   **Color label:** Organizes your images by labeling with a color

R   **Like and Dislike:** Like (heart) or dislike (X) a photo

S   **Rotate:** Click to rotate left or right

T   **Filename:** The image filename and type

STEP BY STEP WITH ON1 PHOTO RAW

THE BROWSE WORKSPACE (RIGHT SIDE)

A   **Image counter:** Displays the number of image files within the folder or album

B   **Info panel:** Displays metadata information about the selected file (also displays the Navigator and Histogram when in Filmstrip view mode)

C   **Metadata panel:** Shows the author's name, description, and keywords for the selected photograph(s)

D   **EXIF & IPTC panels:** Displays detailed information about the selected file (metadata, exposure information, copyright and contact, etc.)

E   **Module selector:** Use to switch to the other modules within ON1 Photo RAW

F   **Export icon:** Click to access the Export section

G   **Share icon:** Click to share a photo online (email, Twitter, Facebook, etc.)

H   **Toggle right section (open/close):** Click to hide or reveal the right sidebar section

I   **Reset All button:** Removes all edits from the Develop and Effects modules

J   **Sync button:** Syncs edits from the Develop and Effects modules across more than one image

DEVELOP

If you are processing Raw photographs inside of ON1 Photo RAW, then the *Develop* module is the first place you will want to go in your workflow. Not only does this module have the basics (white balance and tone adjustments), but it also allows you to add stylization as well.

RAW EDITING

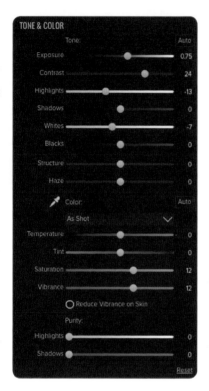

The benefit to photographing in Raw format is that you have a lot more image data to work with within the image file. My favorite part of using Raw files is the ability to perfectly adjust the white balance in post-processing, even if it was photographed incorrectly in-camera. In ON1 Photo RAW you can do this at the bottom of the *Tone & Color* panel on the right.

APPLY ADDITIONAL DEVELOP EFFECTS

If you plan on doing a quick edit of your Raw photo (tone, color, and simple stylizations), then you may want to jump into the additional settings under the *Show More* drop-down at the top of the panel. This allows you to convert to black and white, add a vignette, apply sharpening, remove noise, and more.

LOCAL ADJUSTMENTS

The *Local Adjustments* panel is for when you need to selectively adjust an area, such as adding sharpness to a person's eyes or darkening a too-bright sky. You can add as many local adjustment layers as you would like, and each can be masked separately using either the Brush tool or the Masking Bug.

SIMPLE RETOUCHING & CROPPING

The Develop module is also a good place to clean up the photograph using either the *Retouch Brush* (good for small blemishes and sensor spots) or the *Perfect Eraser* (useful to remove larger items, such as power lines and people). And you can also crop the photo as well using the *Crop* tool on the left.

THE DEVELOP WORKSPACE (LEFT SIDE)

A   **Presets panel:** Applies presets from both Develop and Effects to an image

B   **Tool Options bar:** Displays options from the active tool or brush

C   **Crop tool:** Crops and resizes a photo

D   **Adjustment Brush:** Applies selective edits; works in conjunction with the Local Adjustments panel on the right

E   **Adjustable Gradient:** Applies selective gradients; works in conjunction with the Local Adjustments panel on the right

F   **Perfect Eraser:** Useful for removing larger items within an image

G   **Retouch Brush:** Removes small blemishes and sensor spots

H   **Zoom tool:** Zooms the preview area in and out

I   **Preferences icon:** Click to access the Preferences window

J   **Help Icon:** Click to access the ON1 support website (Internet required)

K   **Toggle left section (open/close):** Click to hide or reveal the left sidebar section

L   **Detail view:** Displays a full-screen photo in the preview area (shown here)

M   **Filmstrip:** Brings up a filmstrip view of your photos at the bottom of the window

N   **Magnification slider:** Zooms the preview image in and out

O   **Compare preview:** Toggles a split before-and-after view of your image

P   **Mask preview:** Toggles the mask preview on and off

Q   **Preview toggle:** Click to toggle between the before and after images

A — Fit 100 50 25

B — NAV

C — HISTO

D — INFO

Fit 100 50 25

OVERALL SETTINGS   LOCAL ADJUSTMENTS — E

SHOW MORE — F

Black & White   Sharpening
Color Adjustment   Skin Retouching
Curves   Split Tone
Glow   Transform
Noise Reduction   Vignette

TONE & COLOR — G

Tone: Auto
Exposure   0.75
Contrast   24
Highlights   -13
Shadows   0
Whites   -7
Blacks   0
Structure   0
Haze   0

Color: Auto
As Shot
Temperature   0
Tint   0
Saturation   12
Vibrance   12
Reduce Vibrance on Skin
Purity:
Highlights   0
Shadows   0
Reset

BROWSE
DEVELOP
EFFECTS
LAYERS
RESIZE

H

I

J

K

Reset All   Reset   Sync

L   M   N

STEP BY STEP WITH ON1 PHOTO RAW

THE DEVELOP WORKSPACE (RIGHT SIDE)

A **Tool Options bar:** Displays options from the active tool or brush

B **Navigator:** Shows the location of the zoomed-in area

C **Histogram:** Displays the histogram of the photograph

D **Info panel:** Displays metadata information about the selected file

E **Overall Settings/Local Adjustments:** Switches between global edits and selective adjustments

F **Show More:** Reveals additional edits that can be made in the Develop module

G **Tone & Color:** The main editing section of the Develop panel; nondestructively edits tone and color (including white balance) of Raw photographs

H **Module selector:** Use to switch to the other modules within ON1 Photo RAW

I **Export icon:** Click to access the Export section

J **Share icon:** Click to share a photo online (email, Twitter, Facebook, etc.)

K **Toggle right section (open/close):** Click to hide or reveal the right sidebar section

L **Reset All button:** Removes all edits from the Develop and Effects modules

M **Reset button:** Removes all edits from only the Develop module

N **Sync button:** Syncs edits from the Develop and Effects modules across more than one image (only in Filmstrip view)

EFFECTS

The *Effects* module is by far my favorite place to go when polishing and adding final touches and stylizations to a photograph. Here you can add simple color and tone corrections, enhance an image with filters and presets, blend textures, add borders, and so much more. You can add global adjustments or selectively edit your photo using either masks or the Local Adjustments section. Here are some of the features of ON1 Effects that stand out and are worth highlighting.

APPLY PRESETS & FILTERS

At its core, ON1 Effects allows you to add a quick preset to your photo or concoct your own creations using one or more filters. There are 23 filters to choose from, and after applying a filter, you can select one of the presets from *within* the filter or change the settings manually. You can also save your own presets to use later (or share with friends), as well as import presets that you purchase or download online.

BLEND AND LAYER FILTERS

The *Filter Stack* is where the magic happens. Each time you add a filter, it is "stacked" in the Filter Stack. The order the filters appear determines how they affect your image. Also, each filter has the ability to be blended with the layers below it. To access these features, click the small gear icon on the top of the individual filter. Then you can use the blending drop-down, as well as the *Apply To* section, to blend the filter with your image. You can also set the filter's individual opacity setting using the slider at the top of this section as well.

ADD A MASK TO ANY FILTER

The Effects module has a *Local Adjustments* section, identical to what you find in the Develop module. However one thing that makes Effects powerful is the ability to mask any of the layers within the Filter Stack using the *Masking Brush* and the *Masking Bug*. These tools allow you to customize your photograph's effects and add them to either the entire image or only a specified (masked) area.

MASTER BLENDING & MASKING

At the top of the Filter Stack are the *Overall Settings*, where you can *globally* change the blending mode and opacity of all filters. Here you can also add a single mask to the entire Filter Stack.

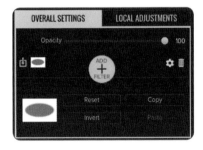

THE EFFECTS WORKSPACE (LEFT SIDE)

A   **Presets panel:** Applies presets from both Develop and Effects to an image

B   **Filters panel:** Lists all filters; also shows a live thumbnail preview of the effect

C   **Tool Options bar:** Displays options from the active tool or brush

D   **Crop tool:** Crops and resizes a photo

E   **Adjustment Brush:** Applies selective edits; works in conjunction with the Local Adjustments panel on the right

F   **Adjustable Gradient:** Applies selective gradients; works in conjunction with the Local Adjustments panel on the right

G   **Masking Brush:** Adds a mask to any filter in the Filter Stack on the right

H   **Masking Bug:** Adds a gradient mask to any filter in the Filter Stack on the right

I   **Refine Brush:** Refines and cleans up an existing mask

J   **Perfect Eraser:** Useful for removing larger items within an image

K   **Retouch Brush:** Removes small blemishes and sensor spots

L   **Zoom tool:** Zooms the preview area in and out

M   **Preferences icon:** Click to access the Preferences window

N   **Help Icon:** Click to access the ON1 support website (Internet required)

O   **Toggle left section (open/close):** Click to hide or reveal the left sidebar section

P   **Detail view:** Displays a full-screen photo in the preview area (shown here)

Q   **Filmstrip:** Brings up a filmstrip view of your photos at the bottom of the window

R   **Magnification slider:** Zooms the preview image in and out

S   **Compare preview:** Toggles a split before-and-after view of your image

T   **Mask preview:** Click to toggle the mask preview on and off

U   **Preview toggle:** Click to toggle between the before and after images

V   **Search bar:** Searches for a specific preset or filter name

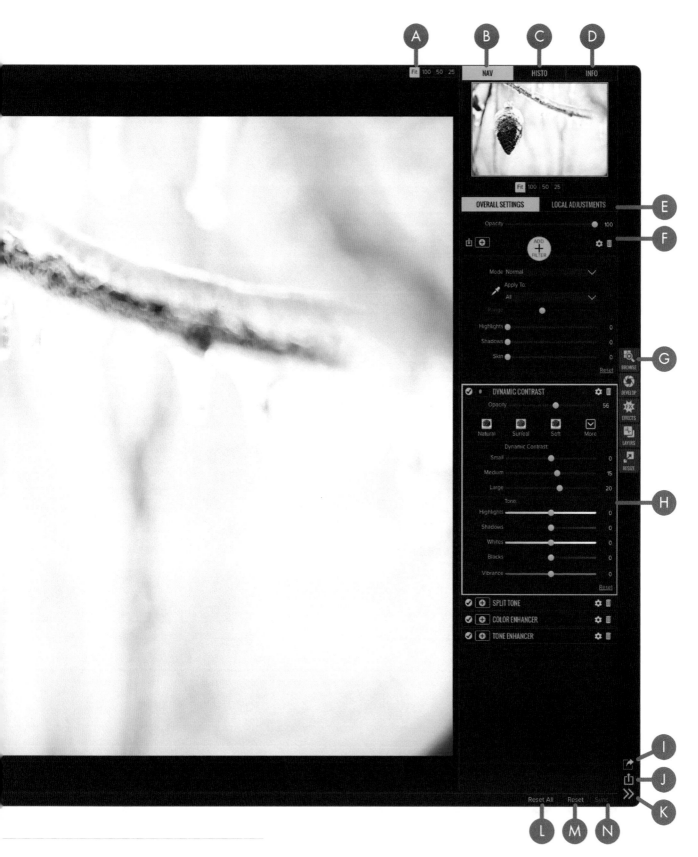

A — Fit 100 50 25
B — NAV
C — HISTO
D — INFO

Fit 100 50 25

OVERALL SETTINGS   LOCAL ADJUSTMENTS — E

Opacity   100
F

ADD
FILTER

Mode   Normal

Apply To:
All

Range
Highlights   0
Shadows   0
Skin   0

Reset

G — BROWSE
DEVELOP
EFFECTS
LAYERS
RESIZE

DYNAMIC CONTRAST
Opacity   56

Natural   Surreal   Soft   More

Dynamic Contrast:
Small   0
Medium   15
Large   20

Tone:
Highlights   0
Shadows   0
Whites   0
Blacks   0
Vibrance   0

Reset   — H

SPLIT TONE
COLOR ENHANCER
TONE ENHANCER

I
J
K

Reset All   Reset   Sync

L   M   N

STEP BY STEP WITH ON1 PHOTO RAW

THE EFFECTS WORKSPACE (RIGHT SIDE)

A   **Tool Options bar:** Displays options from the active tool or brush

B   **Navigator:** Shows the location of the zoomed-in area

C   **Histogram:** Displays the histogram of the photograph

D   **Info panel:** Displays metadata information about the selected file

E   **Overall Settings/Local Adjustments:** Switches between global (Overall Settings) and selective edits (Local Adjustments)

F   **Master Effects settings:** Sets the global opacity, mask, and blending options of all layers in the Filter Stack below (the blending options are only visible by clicking on the gear icon within the panel)

G   **Module selector:** Switches to the other modules within ON1 Photo RAW

H   **Filter Stack:** Displays the filters added to the image

I   **Export icon:** Click to access the Export section

J   **Share icon:** Click to share a photo online (email, Twitter, Facebook, etc.)

K   **Toggle right section (open/close):** Click to hide or reveal the right sidebar section

L   **Reset All button:** Removes all edits from the Develop and Effects modules

M   **Reset button:** Removes all edits from only the Develop module

N   **Sync button:** Syncs edits from the Develop and Effects modules across more than one image (only in Filmstrip view)

LAYERS

When it comes to merging photos and creating any other type of layer-based pixel work, then the *Layers* module is the place to be. Here you can give your photograph a new sky, drop a different background into a portrait, blend textures, and create your composites from elements of more than one photograph. The possibilities go only as far as your own creativity!

MASK WITH EASE

The Layers module's strongest feature set is its ability to quickly create masks. Many of the masking tools depend on a distinct color contrast, so I find it best to work on images that offer me a good starting place, such as a landscape with a blank blue sky or a portrait with a background that is a different color than the person's hair and clothing. Once you create a good starting mask, the Layers module offers even more tools to help refine that mask (my personal favorite is the Chisel tool).

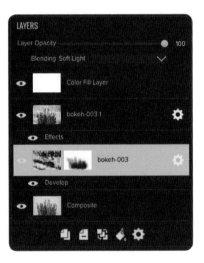

LAYERS & BLENDING

The Layers panel allows you to stack and blend your layers, making the creative possibilities endless. The layers can be blended using the *Opacity* slider and *Blending* setting at the top. To rearrange the layer order, simply drag and drop.

CREATE RE-EDITABLE LAYERS

Another of the Layers module's strengths is that it easily integrates with the other modules, particularly with Develop and Effects. On the bottom of the Layers panel is a gear icon, and by clicking on this icon, you can convert the selected layer into a *Smart Layer*. (You can also right-click on a layer and choose "Convert to Smart Layer.") Then, after editing that same layer in the Develop and/or Effects module, you have the ability to re-edit that photo within those modules at any time in the future. (If you are familiar with Smart Objects in Photoshop , then this is a very similar type of setting.)

QUICKLY ACCESS IMAGE & OVERLAY FILES

On the left side of the application window is a browser where you can access either your own images within their folders on your hard drive or images in the *Extras* folders. Inside the Extras folder, ON1 has provided some default backgrounds, borders, and textures, but you can also add your own using the *Extras Manager* (see below).

THE EXTRAS MANAGER

While not necessarily a part of the Layers module, the *Extras Manager* is where you go when you want to import textures and other downloaded files to use inside of ON1 Layers and also in Effects (borders and textures only). To access this window, go to **File > Manage Extras**, click on the category you would like to import into, and then locate the files on your computer.

THE LAYERS WORKSPACE (LEFT SIDE)

A **Files Browser:** Accesses files on your hard drive or computer

B **Extras Browser:** Accesses extras (backgrounds, borders, and textures)

C **Tool Options bar:** Displays options from the active tool or brush

D **Transform tool:** Moves, transforms, and resizes the selected layer

E **Crop tool:** Crops and resizes a photo

F **Trim tool:** Trims a layer without affecting canvas size

G **Masking Brush:** Adds a mask to the selected layer

H **Quick Mask Brush:** Masks out large areas of similar color and tone

I **Masking Bug:** Adds a gradient mask to the selected layer

J **Line Mask:** Draws a mask using straight lines

K **Refine Brush:** Refines and cleans up an existing mask

L **Chisel Mask:** Removes a small amount of pixels from the edge of a mask

M **Blur Mask:** Blurs the edge of a mask

N **Perfect Eraser:** Useful for removing larger items within an image

O **Retouch Brush:** Removes small blemishes and sensor spots

P **Clone Stamp:** Samples/copies one area and brushes it to another area of a layer

Q **Red Eye:** Removes red eye

R **Hand tool:** Moves the position of a zoomed-in image within the preview area

S **Zoom tool:** Zooms the preview area in and out

T **Preferences icon:** Click to access the Preferences window

U **Help Icon:** Click to access the ON1 support website (Internet required)

V **Toggle left section (open/close):** Click to hide or reveal the left sidebar section

W **Search bar:** Searches the Files and Extras panels

A Fit 100 50 25

B NAV

C LOUPE

D HISTO

E INFO

Zoom ● 100

F LAYERS

Layer Opacity ● 23

Blending Soft Light ⌄

Color Fill Layer

bokeh-003 1 ⚙

Effects

bokeh-003 ⚙

Develop

Composite

G BROWSE
DEVELOP
EFFECTS
LAYERS
RESIZE

H
I
J »

K Close

L Save

THE LAYERS WORKSPACE (RIGHT SIDE)

A   **Tool Options bar:** Displays options from the active tool or brush

B   **Navigator:** Shows the location of the zoomed-in area

C   **Loupe:** Displays a zoomed-in area of the cursor's location

D   **Histogram:** Displays the histogram of the photograph

E   **Info panel:** Displays metadata information about the selected file

F   **Layers panel:** Controls layer order, opacity, and blending modes

G   **Module selector:** Switches to the other modules within ON1 Photo RAW

H   **Export icon:** Click to access the Export section

I   **Share icon:** Click to share a photo online (email, Twitter, Facebook, etc.)

J   **Toggle right section (open/close):** Click to hide or reveal the right sidebar section

K   **Close button:** Closes the document

L   **Save button:** Saves the document

M   **Layer Opacity:** Displays opacity of the selected layer (0 to 100%)

N   **Blending Mode:** Displays the selected layer's blending mode

O   **Layer Visibility:** Shows or hides the layer

P   **Smart Photo indicator:** Indicates that the layer is a re-editable Smart Photo

Q   **Smart Photo modules:** Displays the modules edited with the Smart Photo

R   **Duplicate:** Duplicates the selected layer

S   **Delete:** Deletes the selected layer

T   **Merge:** Merges the selected layer with the layer below

U   **Color Fill:** Adds a color fill layer

V   **Smart Layer:** Converts the selected layer to a Smart Layer

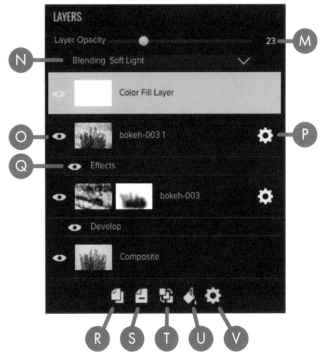

RESIZE

The *Resize* module, formerly known as Genuine Fractals, allows you to resize a photograph (both bigger and smaller), as well as prepare an image for printing. If you plan on using this module then it should be the very last step in your photographic workflow before printing.

RESIZE A DOCUMENT

At its core, Resize allows you to change the pixel dimensions and image ratio of your photograph. It can create high-quality enlargements using ON1's patented algorithms without loss of sharpness or detail. You can also add sharpening and film grain to "polish" the final printed photograph.

CREATE A READY-TO-PRINT GALLERY WRAP

The Resize module allows you to bypass one of the downsides of printing a canvas image, which is having to wrap a portion of the photograph around the canvas frame. Some printing services do not offer this as an option automatically, and it is especially helpful if you are printing on your own device. The *Gallery Wrap* panel will let you choose the wrap's thickness, type of wrap, or even add a solid color instead of mirroring the image border.

SPLIT AN IMAGE INTO TILES

Another fun way to print a photograph is to print it in tiles and then arrange it accordingly on your wall. The *Tiling* panel lets you choose the tile size (I always prefer setting these to columns and rows for the most accurate split), and you can also select the export file type as well.

THE RESIZE WORKSPACE (LEFT SIDE)

A   **Presets panel:** Applies Resize presets

B   **Tool Options bar:** Displays options from the active tool

C   **Crop tool:** Crops and resizes a photo

D   **Hand tool:** Moves the position of a zoomed-in image within the preview area

E   **Zoom tool:** Zooms the preview area in and out

F   **Preferences icon:** Click to access the Preferences window

G   **Help Icon:** Click to access the ON1 support website (Internet required)

H   **Toggle left section (open/close):** Click to hide or reveal the left sidebar section

I   **Search bar:** Searches the Preset panel

PRESETS

Favorites
Canon Canvas
Canon Matte
Canon Resin Coated
Epson Canvas
Epson Matte
Epson Resin Coated
HP Canvas
HP Matte
HP Resin Coated
Photo Lab
Video
Web & Email

Zoom 24.91

CROP
VIEW

Q Search

A — Fit 100 50 25
B — NAV
C — LOUPE
D — HISTO
E — INFO

Fit 100 50 25

F — PIXEL DIMENSIONS

DOCUMENT SIZE
Preset Custom
Width 24   inches
Height 16   inches
Resolution 300   pixels/inch
                    Reset
G

SETTINGS
Image Type General Purpose
Method Genuine Fractals
Texture ————————●——————— 3
Threshold ●——————————————— 25
Smoothness ●————————————— 0
                    Reset
H

I — BROWSE
DEVELOP
EFFECTS
LAYERS
RESIZE

☑ SHARPENING
Type Unsharp Mask
Halo ————●——————————— 2
Amount ●——————————————— 25
Protect:
Highlights ●———————————— 20
Shadows ●———————————— 20
                    Reset
J

○ FILM GRAIN
Amount   ●   Reset
K

○ TILING
Tile Size
Width 8   inches
Height 10   inches
Overlap 0   inches
Output
Tile Count 6
File Type JPEG
Location   Choose
                    Reset
L

☑ GALLERY WRAP
Type Reflect Soft
Thickness 2   inches
Wrap Overlay:
Overlay Color
Opacity ●—————————————— 0
☑ Add To New Layer
                    Reset
M

N
O
P — ≫

Cancel   Done
Q   R

STEP BY STEP WITH ON1 PHOTO RAW

THE RESIZE WORKSPACE (RIGHT SIDE)

A   **Tool Options bar:** Displays options from the active tool

B   **Navigator:** Shows the location of the zoomed-in area

C   **Loupe:** Displays a zoomed-in area of the cursor's location

D   **Histogram:** Displays the histogram of the photograph

E   **Info panel:** Displays metadata information about the selected file

F   **Pixel Dimensions:** Displays the pixel dimensions of the file

G   **Document Size:** View or change the document size in pixels, cm, in, mm, or percent

H   **Settings:** Use to set the image type and resize algorithm when enlarging a photo

I   **Module selector:** Switches to the other modules within ON1 Photo RAW

J   **Sharpening panel:** Use to sharpen your image

K   **Film Grain panel:** Adds film grain to the final resized image

L   **Tiling panel:** Tile the photograph to split into more than one printable document

M   **Gallery Wrap panel:** Adds a wrapped border to the outside edges of the image

N   **Export icon:** Click to access the Export section

O   **Share icon:** Click to share a photo online (email, Twitter, Facebook, etc.)

P   **Toggle right section (open/close):** Click to hide or reveal the right sidebar section

Q   **Cancel button:** Cancels the edits and closes the document without saving

R   **Done button:** Saves and closes the document

PREFERENCES

The *Preferences* window is where you set your general preferences while using the software. It's a good idea to take a look at your settings now and set them accordingly. Here is some advice and tips for a handful of the settings within this window, but please feel free to set them according to your own personal workflow and desires.

GENERAL

The *General* tab is where you set your preferences for the application window and how you interact with it. The first setting, *Working Color Space*, is set by default to *sRGB*. I prefer a larger color space with more color data, however, so I have mine set to *Adobe RGB*.

The *Scrolling Controls* option allows you to choose a behavior for the scroll of your mouse or trackpad. *Preview Zoom* makes the scroll act as a zoom tool, *Preview Pan*

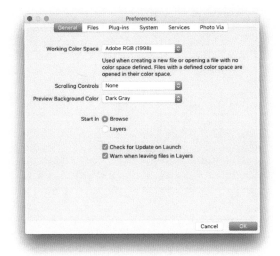

allows you to pan the preview area, and *Brush Size* lets you increase or decrease the size of your brush with the scroll of your mouse when a brush tool is selected.

The *Start In* section allows you to choose which module ON1 Photo RAW will open into when you open the application. If you plan on editing most of your photos from start to finish (as I will be demonstrating in this book), then you will want to select *Browse*. If you prefer to edit existing PSD files inside of ON1 Photo and will not be using it as a Raw processor, then you may want to select the *Layers* option.

FILES

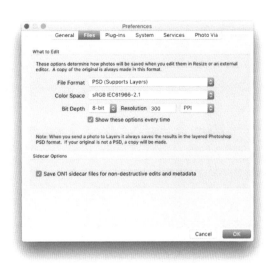

The top section of the *Files* tab, *What to Edit*, allows you to specify the file type for images that are opened into the Resize module or sent to an external editor. Note that these settings do not affect images sent into the Layers module, which will always create a layered PSD version of your photo (if it is not already a PSD, that is).

At the bottom of this window is the *Sidecar Options* section. Leaving this option *unchecked* will keep all edits and processing done in the Develop and/or Effects modules within the application itself. This means that if something were to happen to your application (such as, your hard drive crashes and you lose your application data), then you would also lose the edits you made to your photographs. I prefer to keep this box checked, which saves the processing data in an .ON1 file alongside my images on my external hard drive. The image below shows an example of what this sidecar file will look like alongside an original Raw photograph in the folder view.

PLUG-INS

The *Plug-Ins* tab allows you to choose settings for your photographs when the images are brought in from other sources, such as Lightroom and Photoshop. Under *Smart Photos*, if you would like to make sure that your PSD files processed inside of ON1 Photo are re-editable, then be sure to select the *Smart Photo (Re-editable)* option. Otherwise the edits made in ON1 Photo RAW will be "burned" into the PSD file, and you will not be able to re-edit the file with the original edits still in place.

Under the *Photoshop* settings, you have the option of applying your ON1 edits to either the current layer or a *copy* of the current layer (the option you choose will depend on your personal workflow). For advanced users, if you prefer to use Smart Objects in Photoshop before editing in ON1 Photo, then this option will not affect how the edited layer behaves after it is brought back from ON1 Photo.

At the bottom of this tab are the *Lightroom* settings. If you prefer to edit your Raw photographs in Lightroom and then bring them into ON1 Photo for further stylization, then you will want to make sure you have these options set to your liking. I recommend the *File Type* set to the default (PSD), with the *Color Space* set to Adobe RGB and *Resolution* set at 300 ppi. For the *Bit Depth* setting you have a choice of either 8-bit or 16-bit. The 16-bit option will allow you more data to work with, but this setting will also create a significantly larger file size. Unless you plan on pushing your pixels and doing a massive amount of editing, then you are probably going to be okay with 8-bit (which is the setting I tend to work in most often).

SYSTEM

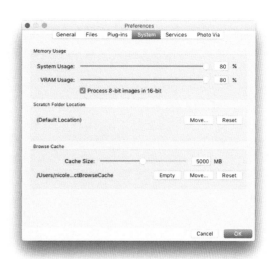

The *System* tab is where you select your settings for memory and cache storage. Under *Memory Usage*, you will likely want to keep these settings as-is. These sliders determine how much memory the ON1 Photo application can use while it is open; setting it too low may prevent the application from functioning properly.

Under *Scratch Folder Location*, set this to your fastest internal hard drive. Again, the default for this may be sufficient for your hardware configuration.

At the bottom is the *Browse Cache* setting, which sets the maximum file size for the previews shown in the Browse module. If you have plenty of space on your hard drive (and have a large photo collection), then you might want to increase the slider so that it is greater than the default setting of 5000 MB. You can also relocate the cache to a different drive, empty it (which will not delete your photos, only the previews it creates), as well as reset it to its default settings.

SERVICES

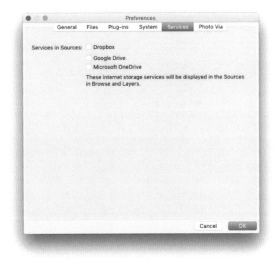

Under the *Services* tab, you have the option of hiding or revealing the Cloud Storage in the Folders section of the Browse module. I don't store my main working files in the cloud, so I prefer to leave these boxes unchecked. Below you can see an example of what it looks like with these services checked (left) and unchecked (right).

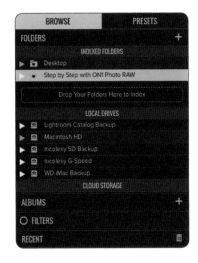

PHOTO VIA

Photo Via is a cloud service used by ON1 Photo that uses either Dropbox or Google Drive to publish and synchronize your photos in the cloud. It works in conjunction with the Photo Via mobile application on iOS and Android, and once it is set up you can view, rate, and share your photos using your mobile device. This service is free, but you do need an account on either Google Drive or Dropbox for it to work.

CHAPTER TWO

EVERYDAY ADJUSTMENTS

ON1 Photo RAW has capabilities to spare. You can easily stylize a photograph and design unique and creative works of art, but sometimes you don't need to go that far. There is a lot of beauty in the subtleties of a simple photograph, and that's where everyday adjustments comes into play.

In this chapter, I will walk through four Raw photographs from start to finish to demonstrate how to properly and effectively use the Develop and Effects modules to change a photograph from "blah" to beautiful. Let's get started!

BASIC RAW EDITS

The power behind ON1 Photo RAW is its ability to nondestructively process a Raw photograph using the Develop module. This module not only allows you to edit the basic tone and white balance of your photo, but it also has additional adjustments that you can Apply. To access these, click the Show More button at the top of the sidebar on the right. In fact, you may even discover that the Develop module is all you need to create a beautifully edited and finished version of your Raw photograph. In this tutorial, I will walk through the steps of editing a photograph solely within the Develop module.

STEP 1

Let's start out by locating the file named *nicolesy-lionfish.cr2* from inside the *Browse* Module. Click on it once to select it, then click the **Develop** icon at the top of the *Module Selector* on the far right to open it into the Develop module.

STEP 2

This image was photographed underwater and is in sore need of color correction to remove the blue-green color cast. Because it is a Raw file, I am able to correct the white balance without degrading the overall quality of the image.

To do this, I access the *Color* section at the bottom of the panel and slide the **Temperature** to **180**. This adds warmth to the image and removes the blue color cast. Then, I move the **Tint** slider to **140** to add magenta and correct for the existing green color cast.

STEP 1

STEP 2

STEP 3

Next, I move my attention to the *Tone* section at the top of the panel. I set the **Exposure** to **1.8** to add brightness, and I increase the overall contrast by moving the **Contrast** slider to **24**.

The exposure adjustment created some overly bright areas in the eye of the fish, so to compensate I move the **Highlights** slider to **-30**. I also slide the **Shadows** to **14** to bring some detail back into the darker areas of the image.

STEP 4

I would like to add some more contrast to the image, and to do this I will use a curve. In the *Overall Settings* at the top, I click the **Show More** button and select **Curves** from the list.

In the new panel that appears, I create a subtle s-curve. To do this, I click over the line in the upper-right quadrant, drag the line slightly upwards, and then click over the line in the lower-left quadrant and drag it slightly downwards. The line is now a subtle "S" shape, adding subtle contrast to the image.

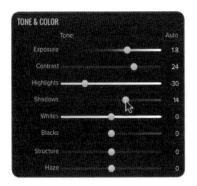

STEP 3

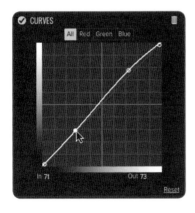

STEP 4

STEP 5

Now I would like to clean up the small particles that are floating around the fish. I select the **Retouch Brush** from the toolbar, and then go to the options at the top and set the brush's **Size** to **45**. Next, I click over each of the little dots in the image to clean it up. I also resize the brush as needed using the [and] (bracket) keys. (The example photo on the right shows a 100% zoomed-in before-and-after view.)

STEP 6

In the top-left corner of the image is a dark area that I would like to remove. To begin I select the **Perfect Eraser** from the toolbar, zoom in to 100%, and then pan to that corner so that I can see it more clearly.

Next, I set the Perfect Eraser's **Size** to **200** and make a big sweep over the dark spot, making sure to also include some of the green background that I want the dark spot to be replaced with.

Note: You may need to undo and repeat this process a couple of times before you get a good fill of the area you want to replace.

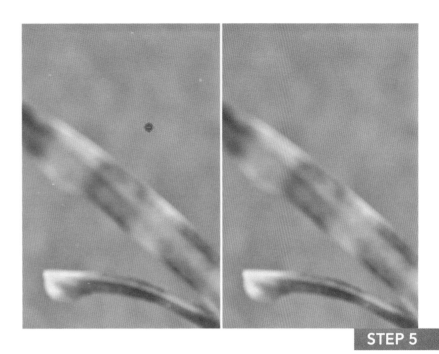

STEP 5

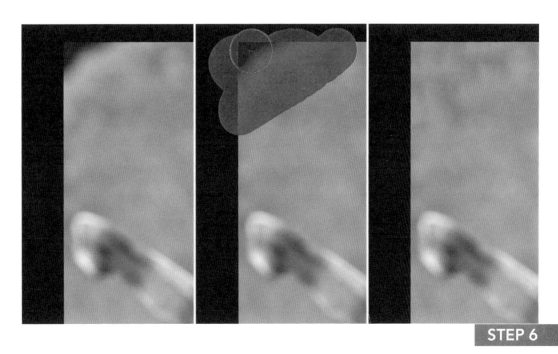

STEP 6

STEP 7

Now I would like to make some adjustments to only the eye of the fish. To do this I will use the **Local Adjustments** tab at the top. I click it once to activate the panel, and the **Adjustment Brush** is automatically selected in the toolbar.

Next, in the options at the top, I make sure that the **Mode** is set to **Paint In**, I set the **Size** to **200**, set both the **Feather** and **Opacity** sliders to **100%**, and then brush over the eye of the fish. I also reset the **Exposure** slider to **0** and increase the **Shadows** to **30** and **Detail** to **12**. This adds a touch of sharpening and shadow detail to the eyes.

STEP 8

There is some visible noise in the image, so I head back to the *Overall Adjustments* section. There, I click the **Show More** button and choose **Noise Reduction** from the list.

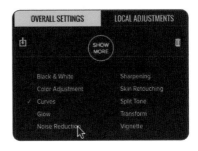

In the panel that appears below, I select the **Subtle** preset, which removes a small amount of noise without smudging the fine details in the fish.

STEP 7

STEP 8

STEP 9

For the last step I would like to add a vignette. I click the **Show More** button at the top and choose **Vignette** from the list.

Then, in the panel below, I choose the **Big Softy** preset. This adds a beautiful soft and dark vignette, helping to bring attention to the center of the image.

BEFORE

AFTER

BLACK & WHITE

There are many reasons that you may want to do a black-and-white conversion. Maybe the color version of the original is dull and unnecessary, or perhaps the photo has a strong subject that is best displayed in monochrome. With this photograph, changing it to black and white using the Develop module will give it a timeless feel, and also by pulling out the color I will be able to direct the viewer's eyes towards the action and emotion within the photograph.

STEP 1

I begin by locating the file named *nicolesy-bw.raf* from inside the *Browse* module, and then click on it once to select it. On the far right, I click the **Develop** module icon at the top of the module selector to bring the photo into the Develop module.

STEP 2

Next, near the top of the right sidebar, I click the **Show More** button and click **Black & White** to quickly convert the image to black and white.

STEP 1

STEP 2

STEP 3

Now that I can see the image with no color, it will be easier to adjust the tones accordingly. The basic conversion left the image looking flat, so I start out in the *Tone & Color* panel where I increase the **Exposure** to **0.65** and the **Contrast** to **12**.

Then, I move the **Blacks** slider to **-15** to deepen the shadow areas in the image, which also adds more contrast. I move the **Haze** slider to **28**, which adds a touch of glow to the background.

STEP 4

Next, I turn my attention to the *Black & White* panel. This panel uses the colors in the original photograph to increase or decrease the luminosity of those color areas.

I start out by clicking the **Red** filter, which brightens the reds and yellows in the photo. This image has a lot of pink in the girl's clothes, so the filter does a good job of adding brightness to that part of the scene, as well as to her skin tone.

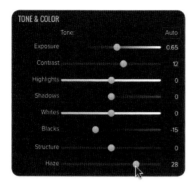

STEP 3

STEP 4

STEP 5

Now I would like to apply a small amount of film grain to the photo, so I head down to the **Film Grain** section of the *Black & White* panel. I select the **Ilford® Delta 400** preset, which adds a nice amount of grain and gives me a good starting point.

The film grain size is a little too large, so I reduce the **Size** slider to **66**. This makes each of the individual film grains smaller.

STEP 6

Next I would like to add a vignette, but I would like to customize the exact location and shape of it. To do this, I first click **Local Adjustments** at the top.

Then, in the toolbar, I activate the **Adjustable Gradient** tool. At the top in the options, I set the **Preset** to **Vignette** and the **Shape** to **Edges**. Next I click on the little girl, which adds the gradient to the layer. I resize the shape of the gradient by clicking and dragging the solid line, and I reposition it with the smaller circle near the center of the mask. This positions the masked area so that it is within the confines of the shape of the little girl.

Finally, over in the **Adjustment** panel, I set the **Exposure** to **-0.7** and the **Highlights** to **-12**, which darkens the area surrounding the little girl.

STEP 5

STEP 6

STEP 7

Lastly, I would like to finish it off by adding a subtle glow to the image. I go back to the *Overall Settings* tab, click **Show More**, and select **Glow**.

Inside the *Glow* panel, I click the **Normal** preset. The effect is too harsh, so I reduce the **Amount** slider to **15**.

BEFORE

AFTER

PORTRAIT

ON1 Photo RAW is a great place to edit portraits. In previous versions of the software, there was an entire module dedicated to processing portrait images. Now many of the features from that module have been integrated with Effects. In this tutorial, I will take the image through the Develop and Effects modules to demonstrate refinements such as removing blemishes, brightening teeth, and enhancing the eyes.

STEP 1

I start by locating the *nicolesy-portrait.dng* file from inside of the *Browse* module. Then I click the **Develop** icon on the right to open the image into the Develop module.

STEP 2

In the *Develop* module, I'll begin by adjusting the tone and color. The overall exposure for this image is quite good, so only a small amount of adjusting is required.

In the *Tone* section at the top, I increase the **Contrast** to **7** to add contrast, and I also increase the **Shadows** to **9** to brighten some of the darker areas of the image.

Then, in the *Color* section, I reduce the **Temperature** slider to **-5** and the **Tint** to **-16**. This applies a subtle correction to the overall white balance.

STEP 1

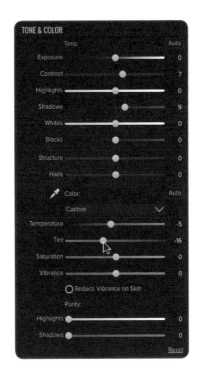

STEP 2

STEP 3

Now I would like to clean up some of the blemishes and other spots in the image. I select the **Retouch Brush** from the toolbar, make sure that the **Feather** is set to **30** and the **Opacity** is set to **100**, and then I resize the brush to be just a little bit larger than the blemish I want to remove. (I do this quickly by using the keyboard shortcuts **[** and **]**, to either decrease or increase the brush size.) I zoom in to 100% and then click once over each blemish to remove it.

I focus my efforts on the blemishes on the skin, the dark specks of makeup under her eyes, cracks in the lipstick, and any other dots outside of the face that are unnecessary to the photograph (dust on the hat and spots on the glasses).

STEP 4

Now I would like to soften the dark creases under her eyes. With the **Retouch Brush** still active, I reduce the brush's **Opacity** to **20%** in the options at the top and set the **Size** to **90**. Next, I pan over to the eyes and sweep the Retouch Brush over the crease beneath her lower eyelid. I do this several times on each side until the crease is faded, but not completely gone.

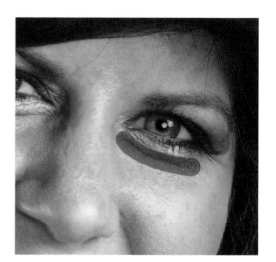

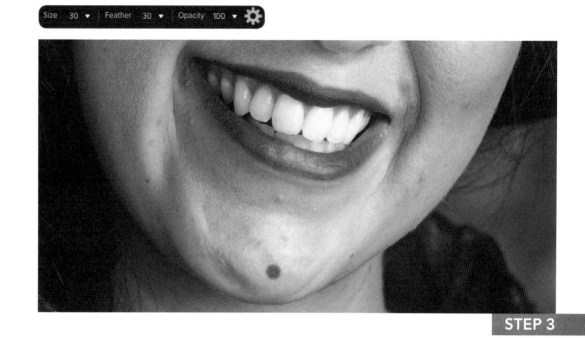

Size 30 ▼ Feather 30 ▼ Opacity 100 ▼

STEP 3

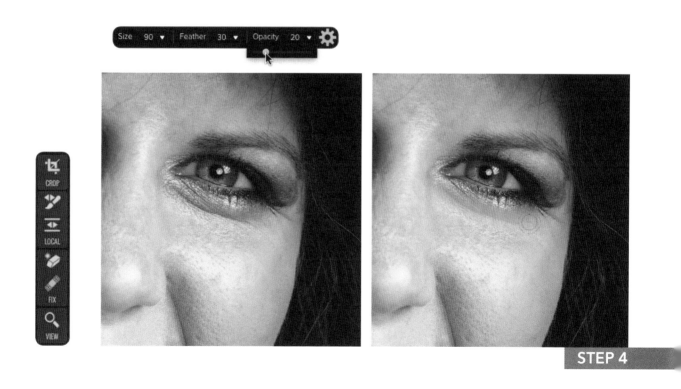

Size 90 ▼ Feather 30 ▼ Opacity 20 ▼

STEP 4

STEP 5

I repeat the process used in *Step 4*, but this time I am focusing on the creases around her mouth. I keep all of the Retouch Brush settings intact and make several brush strokes over the creases to soften them.

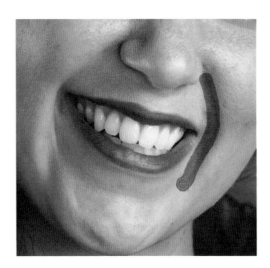

STEP 6

To apply selective edits to small areas of the photo, I click the **Local Adjustments** tab and then reset the **Exposure** slider to **0**. I first want to brighten the teeth, and so I start by zooming in to that area. Then, I go to **Mask > View Mode**, and make sure that **Red Overlay** is selected.

Next, I press the **O** key to preview the mask. In the options at the top, I make sure that I the brush **Mode** is set to **Paint In** and the **Feather** is set to **100**. I also change my brush's size as needed while painting by using the left and right bracket keys.

When I'm finished masking, I press the **O** key again to hide the red mask preview.

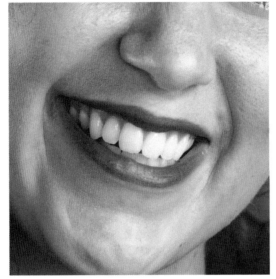

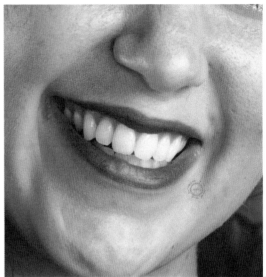

STEP 5

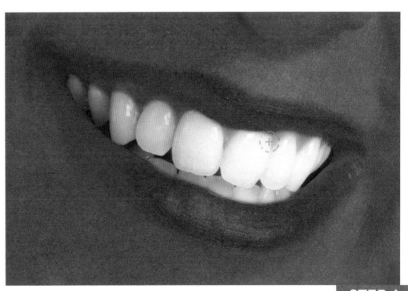

STEP 6

STEP 7

Now in the *Adjustment* panel, I increase the **Exposure** to **0.07** and the **Contrast** to **22**. This adds a small amount of brightness to the teeth without making them look unnatural.

I also decrease the **Temperature** to **-12**, as well as decrease both the **Saturation** and **Vibrance** sliders to **-16**, which removes some of the yellow color cast in the teeth.

STEP 8

Next, I will make some local edits to the eyes. I click the **Add Layers** button at the top, reset the **Exposure** to **0**, and pan over to the eyes.

I maintain the same brush settings as in *Step 6*, press the **O** key to preview the mask, and brush over the eye area. I also make sure to include the eyeshadow areas above and below her eyes in my masked selection.

When I'm finished masking, I press the **O** key again to hide the mask preview.

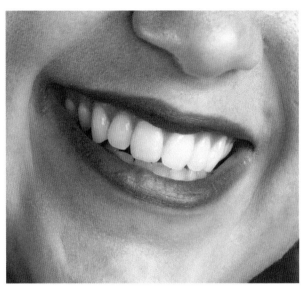
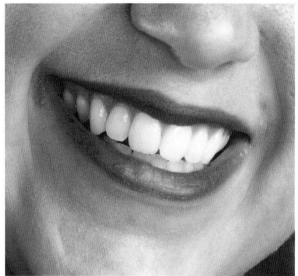

STEP 7

STEP 8

STEP 9

Next I make some adjustments to the sliders in the *Adjustments* panel. I would like to add brightness and contrast to the eyes, so I increase the **Exposure** to **0.2** and the **Contrast** to **20**.

I increase the **Detail** slider to **10**, which adds a sharpening effect to those areas.

I also want to intensify the color of the eyes, so I start by increasing the **Temperature** to **22** to add warmth, and then I increase the **Saturation** to **40**.

These settings give the eyes a nice colorful and contrasty "punch" to help draw attention to those areas of her face.

STEP 10

I would like to apply the skin retouching effect, and this option is available in both the Develop and the Effects modules. The difference between the two modules is that the Skin Retouching filter in Effects can be masked, while the one in the Develop module affects the image globally. I prefer to have more control over the application of the skin retouching effect, so I click the **Effects** icon in the module selector to open the image in Effects.

Once the image is in Effects, I start by clicking the **Overall Settings** tab at the top, and then click **Add Filter**. Then I choose the **Skin Retouching** filter from the list.

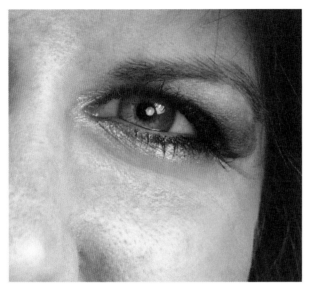

STEP 9

STEP 10

STEP 11

The first thing I need to do is set the skin tone color so that the filter knows which areas are skin and where to apply the settings. To do this, I select the **eyedropper** icon within the filter panel, and then click on the woman's face to choose a skin color. Then I increase the **Range** to **200**, which selects as much of that skin color in the image as it can locate.

STEP 12

The default settings of this filter are quite intense, so I need to adjust all of the sliders to make this look more natural. I begin by reducing the **Blemishes** to **10** and the **Smoothing** to **0**.

There is some shine in the face that I would like to remove, and so I do that by increasing the **Shine** slider to **80**.

I also set the **Evenness** slider to **0** to prevent the filter from affecting the colors in her face.

STEP 12

STEP 13

This filter is affecting more than just the skin in the image, so I will use masking to make sure that only the face area is included in this adjustment.

I start by pressing the **B** key to activate the **Masking Brush**. Then, at the top-right area of the screen, I click **Invert** to invert the mask and hide the filter's effect. I also press the **O** key to toggle the mask preview.

In the brush's options at the top, I make sure that the **Mode** is set to **Paint In** and both the **Feather** and **Opacity** are set to **100**. Then I brush over the skin on the face to reveal the filter effects over only that area.

When I'm finished I press the **O** key again to hide the mask preview.

STEP 14

Now I'm going to add a few more filters in Effects to stylize the photo. I click the **Add Filter** button at the top, and then select **Blur**.

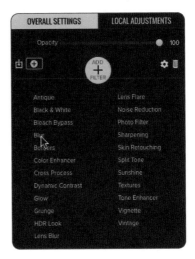

Then, in the filter panel, I click on the **gear** icon to reveal the blending options. Here I change the **Mode** to **Soft Light**, which blends the blur effect with the image, giving it a soft, glowing look. The overall result is too intense, so I reduce the **Opacity** of this filter to **20%**.

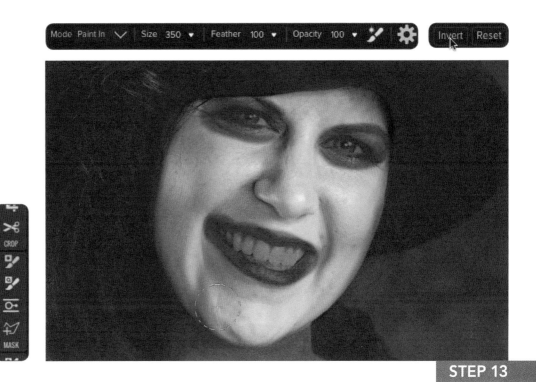

STEP 13

STEP 14

STEP 15

I again click the **Add Filter** button, and this time I choose **Sunshine** from the list. I select the **Natural** preset in the filter panel, and then reduce the filter's **Opacity** to **50%** to soften the effect.

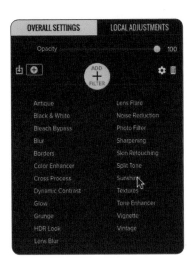

STEP 16

Next I would like to add some sharpening to the photo, but only to the eyes and the mouth. So I start by clicking **Add Filter**, and then I choose the **Sharpening** filter.

In the filter panel, I click the **More** drop-down and select the **Portrait Sharpen** preset. Then I select the **Brush** tool by pressing **B**, and click **Invert** at the top to invert the mask and hide the filter's effect. I also make sure that the brush's **Mode** is set to **Paint In** and the **Opacity** is set to **100%**. Then I sweep over the eyes and mouth to apply the sharpening filter to only those areas.

STEP 15

STEP 16

85

STEP 17

Lastly, I'll add a vignette. I click the **Add Filter** button, and choose the **Vignette** filter.

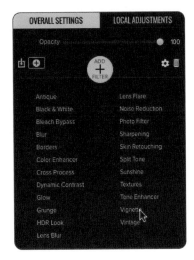

In the filter panel, I select the **Strong** preset to add a nice dark edge to the photo.

I'm finished with this portrait image, so I click the **Browse** icon on the right to bring the photo back into the Browse module.

BEFORE

AFTER

LANDSCAPE

Photographing landscapes is one of my favorite subjects, and ON1 Photo makes it easy to process the photos to look their best. In this example I will bring a photograph of a tulip field into both Develop and Effects to add contrast, color, and some finishing touches.

STEP 1

I begin by locating the *nicolesy-tulips.raf* file inside of the *Browse* module and click on it once to select it. Then, on the far right, I click the **Develop** module icon at the top of the *Module Selector* to bring the photo into the Develop module.

STEP 2

Next I would like to bring out some of the detail in the shadow areas between the rows of tulips. To do this, I go into the *Tone* section and increase the **Shadows** slider to **38** and the **Blacks** slider to **10**.

STEP 1

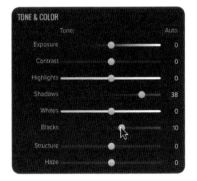

STEP 2

STEP 3

Now it's time to correct the white balance. The image looks pretty good out of camera, but I would like to add some warmth. So in the *Color* section, I increase the **Temperature** slider to **14** and reduce the **Tint** slider to **-6**.

STEP 4

This image is already quite saturated, and I want to make sure that the reds in the photo don't end up looking unnatural. At the same time, I would like to intensify the blue of the sky. I will do this by using the Color Adjustment panel.

At the top, I click **Show More** and select **Color Adjustment** from the list. Then, in the *Color Adjustment* panel, I click the **Sky** preset. This helps deepen the blues in the sky, but I still need to address the bright red color in the tulips.

So I click once over the **Red** color swatch, and then move the **Saturation** to **-10**. Now my sky is blue, and the tulips are no longer oversaturated.

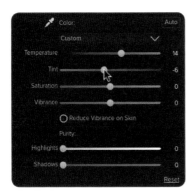

STEP 3

STEP 4

STEP 5

Next I would like to open this image into Effects to add some filters and other stylizations. To do this, I click once on the **Effects** icon over on the right.

I click the **Add Filter** button in the *Overall Settings* tab, and choose the **Color Enhancer** filter. I select the **Sky** preset at the top of this filter, and then near the bottom of this panel, I set the **Hue** slider to **-12**, which slightly alters the color of the blue sky.

STEP 6

I add another color adjustment by clicking the **Add Filter** button and again choosing the **Color Enhancer** filter.

This time I would like to increase the color of the green leaves and stems of the tulips. So I select the **Foliage** preset from the top and leave all of the settings as-is. This does a nice job of bringing the foliage back to a more natural green color.

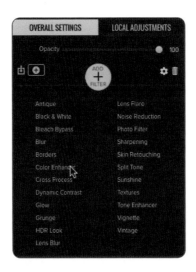

STEP 5

STEP 6

STEP 7

Next, I again add a new filter to the Filter Stack, but this time I select the **Dynamic Contrast** filter. This is a great filter for landscapes as it adds a type of contrast that can be subtle but also give the appearance of sharpening the photograph at the same time.

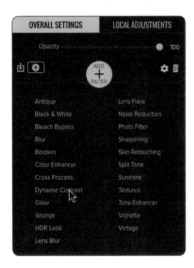

In the presets at the top I select **Soft**, but the effect is overpowering for this photograph. To correct it I reduce the **Opacity** slider of this panel to **25%**.

STEP 8

Another filter I like to use is the Sunshine filter because it adds a beautiful brightness and glow and is a great filter for a wide variety of photographs. So, I add a new filter and choose **Sunshine** from the list.

Then, in the panel options, I select the **Strong** preset. The effect is, as I expected, too strong, so I reduce the **Amount** slider down to **40**.

STEP 7

STEP 8

STEP 9

One other favorite filter of mine is the Polarizer filter. I add a new filter and then select **Photo Filter** from the list.

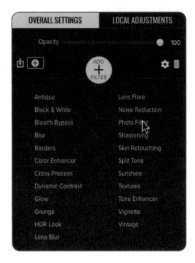

Then, using the **More** drop-down in the *Photo Filter* panel, I select **Polarizer**. This filter is quite intense, so I reduce the **Opacity** to **50%**.

STEP 10

I'd like to add a vignette, but instead of using Effects, I'll head back to the Develop module. So, I click the **Develop** icon on the right, click **Show More** at the top and choose **Vignette** from the list. In the *Vignette* panel, I choose the **Subtle** preset. Next I use the **Type** drop-down and change it to **Normal**. This gives my image a soft vignette along the edges of the photo.

STEP 9

STEP 10

STEP 11

This image could also use some sharpening. Although I am unable to make the photo be perfectly in focus, I can make it *appear* to be more sharp.

I click the **Show More** drop-down and choose **Sharpening**. Then, I select the **Fix Focus** filter and reduce the **Amount** to **30**.

To finish it off, in the **Protect** section of this panel, I set the **Shadows** slider to **64** to prevent the dark areas from being affected by this sharpening filter.

BEFORE

AFTER

CHAPTER
THREE

LAYERS & MASKING

The beauty of working in ON1 Photo is that it has a powerful masking module: the Layers module. Here you can create composites, replace skies, blend layers together, add colored backgrounds, resize layers and documents, and so much more. Another benefit to using this module is that the masks and simple layers are cross-compatible with Photoshop, which means that you can open PSD files in Photoshop that were created in ON1 Photo and vice-versa. I won't be demonstrating that in this tutorial, but it is a good bit of knowledge to store away in case you would like to go back and forth between the applications or you would like to start a mask in ON1 Photo and finish it in Photoshop (for example).

In this chapter, I will walk through three different photographs, demonstrating several masking and layering techniques. We will also jump into some of the other modules as well. Let's get to it!

SKY REPLACEMENT

When photographing landscapes we are not always lucky enough to get a beautiful sky as our backdrop. The good news is that ON1 Photo is an excellent place to go when you would like to spruce up a boring sky by swapping it out with a new one. In this tutorial, I will take a photo I created in Moab, Utah, and give it a beautiful sunset makeover using the Develop, Layers, and Effects modules.

STEP 1

I begin by clicking the file named *nicolesy-moab.raf* from inside the *Browse* module to select it. On the far right, I click the **Develop** icon at the top of the *Module Selector* to bring the photograph into the Develop module.

STEP 2

In the Develop module, I want to make some subtle adjustments to the tone and color. I start in the *Tone* section, where I increase the **Contrast** to **9**, the **Shadows** to **15**, and the **Whites** to **13**. This adds a nice amount of brightness and contrast to the photo.

In the *Color* section, I increase the **Temperature** to **16** to add some warmth, and I remove the slight magenta cast by reducing the **Tint** slider to **-7**.

Then, I click the **Browse** icon on the right to go back into the Browse module.

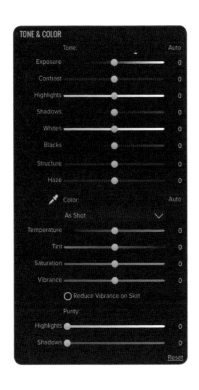

STEP 1

STEP 2

STEP 3

Now I would like to access the new sky I will be adding to the Moab photograph. In the *Browse* module, I click on the *nicolesy-sky. dng* file, and then click once on the **Develop** icon on the right.

STEP 4

I need to add brightness to this sky so that it matches the tones in the Moab image. So, I start out in the *Tone* section and increase the **Exposure** to **1.55**, the **Contrast** to **16**, **Shadows** to **6**, and the **Whites** slider to **13**.

In the *Color* section, I adjust the white balance by increasing the **Temperature** to **16** and reducing the **Tint** to **-12**.

I also notice a small dot in the middle of the image, which looks like a faraway airplane. To fix this, I select the **Retouch Brush** from the toolbar, zoom in to **100%**, and make a short sweep over the blemish to remove it. When I'm finished, I click the **Browse** icon in the *Module Selector*.

STEP 3

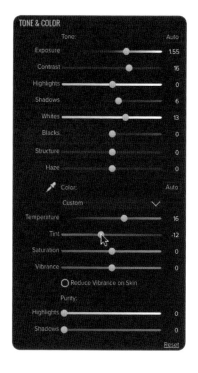

STEP 4

STEP 5

I'm ready to bring these images into the Layers panel, so inside of Browse I select both images by clicking on the *nicolesy-moab.raf* file, and then I press and hold the **Cmd** (PC: **Ctrl**) key to highlight and select the *nicolesy-sky.dng* file as well.

With both images selected, I click the **Layers** icon in the *Module Selector*, and a window pops up asking "Do you want to add this photo as a layer, or open it as a new photo?" I select **Add as Layer**, and the two images open into the Layers module, with each photo on its own layer.

Note: Make sure that you do not already have an image already open in the Layers panel. This method will add those photos as new layers to any open document in Layers.

STEP 6

In the *Layers* panel, I would like to rename each layer to keep things organized. I double-click on the name next to the bottom (landscape) layer and change its name to *Moab*. For the top sky image, I double-click over the name and rename it to *Sky*.

Next I need to reposition these layers so that the *Moab* layer is on top. To do this, I click and drag the *Moab* layer so that it is above the *Sky* layer in the Layers panel.

STEP 5

STEP 6

STEP 7

I'm ready to start masking, and because this image has a large area of similar color and contrast, I will try masking it out all at once. To do this, I select **Quick Mask** from the toolbar and then make a big squiggle over the sky area. ON1 processes the selection and masks out colors that are similar to the ones that I brushed across.

STEP 8

The edge of the mask is still showing some of the original sky, so to fix this I select the **Refine Brush** from the toolbar and make sure that the **Size** is set to **250**. Then I sweep the brush across the entire edge of the mask to remove the remaining bits of pale blue sky.

STEP 7

STEP 8

STEP 9

There is still a slight halo surrounding a lot of the image, so that needs to be addressed. In the next step I will use the Chisel Mask tool to address this, but first I need to "protect" the brushes and branches from being negatively affected by the chiseling.

First, I zoom in to the bottom-left area where there is some green foliage and brush, and select the **Blur Mask** tool from the toolbar. I set the **Amount** to **5** and then make three or four sweeps over this area to blur the edge of the mask. I repeat this step on the foliage on the right side of the image.

Note: This is necessary to prevent the Chisel Mask tool in the next step from removing too many thin branches from the bushes, and also to help make the transition in this area look more natural.

STEP 10

Now I select the **Chisel Mask** tool from the toolbar, and at the top I make sure that the **Amount** is set to **1**. I would like to apply this brush to the entire edge of the mask, so to do this quickly, I double-click this tool in the toolbar. Then, I double-click it once again, and the halo around my mask is now gone.

STEP 9

STEP 10

STEP 11

There is a concrete path showing in my scene, and I would like to crop it out. I select the **Crop** tool from the toolbar, and at the top in the drop-down I select **Original Ratio**.

Next, I click and drag the bottom-right corner until the pathway is no longer visible.

STEP 12

I'm finished masking the photo, so now it's time to bring the image into Effects to further correct the color and give it some stylization. But first I need to create a merged composite layer of both the *Moab* and *Sky* layers.

To do this, I right-click over the top *Moab* layer and choose **New Stamped Layer** Ⓐ. This creates a new merged layer at the top of the Layers panel, leaving the original layers untouched.

I then click on the **gear icon** at the bottom of the Layers panel to convert this new layer into a *Smart Layer* Ⓑ, which gives it the ability to be re-edited after it has been processed in Effects and Develop.

With this new layer still selected, I click the **Effects** icon on the right to open it into the Effects module.

STEP 11

STEP 12

STEP 13

Now I'm in Effects, and it's time to add some filters. I click the **Add Filter** button in the *Overall Settings* tab and select the **Tone Enhancer** filter.

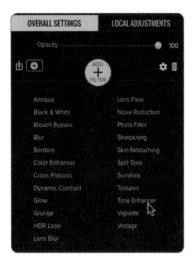

Then, in the filter options, I use the **More** drop-down to bring up some of the filter's presets. From this list I choose the **Tonal Contrast** preset, which helps to bring out the texture in the rocks. I reduce the layer's **Opacity** to **20%** to soften the effect.

STEP 14

I click the **Add Filter** button again, and this time I choose the **Color Enhancer** filter. Next, I use the **More** drop-down in the filter's options to select the **Foliage** preset, which intensifies the greens in the bushes at the bottom of the frame. The overall image has a very magenta color cast to it, so I also reduce the **Tint** slider to **-55** to balance the colors in the photo.

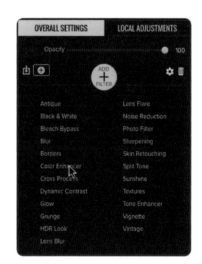

STEP 13

STEP 14

115

STEP 15

Now I would like to add some film grain to this image. The Film Grain setting is hiding in the Black & White filter, and while I don't want to convert this image to black and white, I do have a workaround.

I start out by adding a new filter, and click **Black & White**. Then, in the filter options, I click the **gear icon** on the top-right of the panel ⓒ, which reveals the blending options. In the **Mode** drop-down I choose **Luminosity** ⓓ. This retains the color of the image and applies only the tonal qualities of the black-and-white layer.

Next, I go down to the *Film Grain* section of this panel, select the **Ilford® XP2 Super 400** preset, and then reduce the **Size** slider down to **62**. This adds a nice and subtle film grain effect, which helps blend the sky layer with the landscape to make the composite image appear more realistic.

STEP 16

For the last step I would like to add a vignette. I click the **Add Filter** button and choose **Vignette** from the list.

Then, I select the **Subtle** preset from inside the filter options, reduce the **Size** to **18**, and increase the **Feather** to **100**.

I am now finished with this image, so I click **Done** on the bottom-right of the application window. This opens the photo back into Layers, where I save and close the file.

BEFORE

AFTER

MAGAZINE COVER EFFECT

Playing around with photos in post-processing software can be a lot of fun, and it's also a good way to discover new techniques while creating something impressive. For this tutorial, I will be using a photo of my dog, Kodak, when he was a puppy, and transform him into a celebrity by adding him to the cover of a magazine!

Note: ON1 Photo does not have a text editor within the program, so I created the overlay for this tutorial using Adobe Photoshop.

STEP 1

The photo I am using is a Raw file, so I will first need to process it before I start masking. I click on the *nicolesy-puppy.dng* file inside of *Browse*, and then click the **Develop** icon on the right. This opens the photo into the Develop module.

STEP 2

I start by correcting the tone to make the image brighter with more contrast. First I increase the **Exposure** to **0.75** and **Contrast** to **10**, and then I reduce the **Highlights** to **-70** in order to bring back some of the lost detail in the white fur.

I also increase the **Shadows** to **7** to bring a slight amount of detail into the face.

Then I reduce the **Blacks** slider to **-26** which adds even more contrast to the photo.

STEP 1

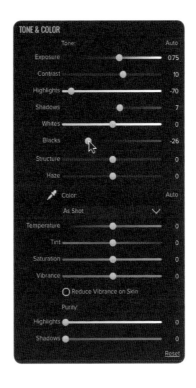

STEP 2

STEP 3

Next I need to add a subtle adjustment to the white balance. In the *Color* section, I increase the **Temperature** to **7** and decrease the **Tint** to **-6**, which helps balance the colors and add warmth to the photo.

STEP 4

I zoom in to the photo and notice some crusts under Kodak's eye on the left, and also some fuzz on the left side of his head.

To fix this, I select the **Perfect Eraser** from the toolbar, set the size to be slightly larger than the area I want to remove, and brush over those two areas. This action clones out the blemishes and replaces them with similar content surrounding the erased area.

I'm finished editing this Raw photo, so I click the **Browse** icon in the module selector to go back into the Browse module.

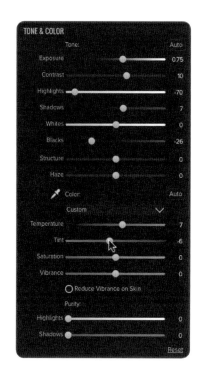

STEP 3

STEP 4

STEP 5

Next, I locate the *nicolesy-magazine.png* file. This is an image that I created inside of Photoshop on a transparent background, and saved as a PNG to preserve the transparency. I want to make sure that my finished file remains the same size as this PNG file, so I will open it first.

I select the magazine image in *Browse*, and then click **Layers** on the right. The image then opens up into the Layers module.

I click the **Browse** icon in the module selector to go back into Browse. This action does not close the magazine file it will remain open in Layers during the next step.

STEP 6

Back inside of *Browse*, I locate the *nicolesy-puppy.dng* file and click the **Layers** icon in the *Module Selector*.

A window pops up asking how I would like to open this file. I already have the magazine document open, so I choose **Add as Layer** to add the puppy photo as a layer to my opened magazine document.

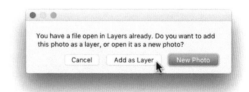

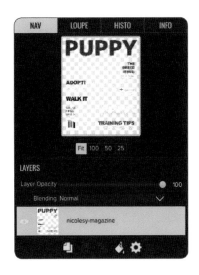

STEP 5

STEP 6

STEP 7

Before moving any further, I would like to rename the layers to better organize my workflow. I double-click the text to the right of the thumbnail and type in the new names. I name the top layer to *Puppy* and the bottom layer to *Magazine*.

Next, I relocate the *Puppy* layer by dragging and dropping so that it is below the *Magazine* layer. Now I am able to see both the magazine overlay and the puppy photo in the image preview area.

STEP 8

I make sure that the *Puppy* layer is active in the Layers panel, and then I select the **Transform** tool. I click and drag the image until it is centered in the frame, with a portion of the ears still covered by the magazine title text at the top.

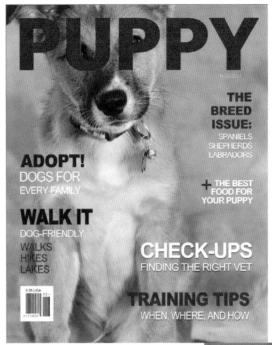

STEP 7

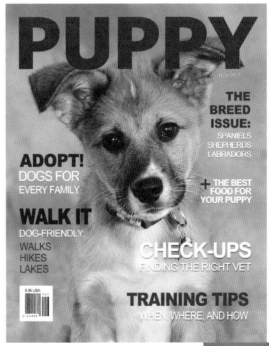

STEP 8

STEP 9

Next I would like to mask the image so that the ears are covering up a portion of the magazine title text. Before I do this, I first need to create a copy of this layer. So with the *Puppy* layer active in the Layers panel, I click the **Duplicate Layer** icon on the bottom of the Layers panel.

STEP 10

With this new copied layer still active in the Layers panel, I drag and drop it so that it is the top layer. This action covers all of the layers below, hiding the magazine overlay.

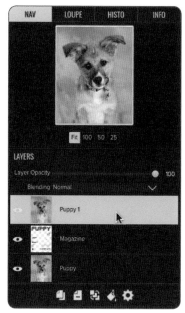

STEP 10

STEP 11

The final step in this process is to do some masking. I select the **Masking Brush** icon from the toolbar, and with the top layer active, I click the **Invert** button on the top-right area of the application window. This creates a black mask next to the layer's thumbnail, hiding this top layer.

Next I use the shortcut **Cmd+R** (PC: **Ctrl+R**) to activate the **Perfect Brush**, make sure that my **Mode** is set to **Paint In**, and then I brush over the head and ears of the puppy in the areas where they are overlapping the letters.

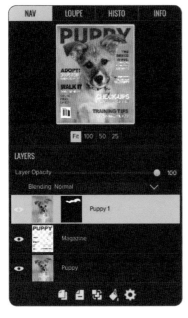

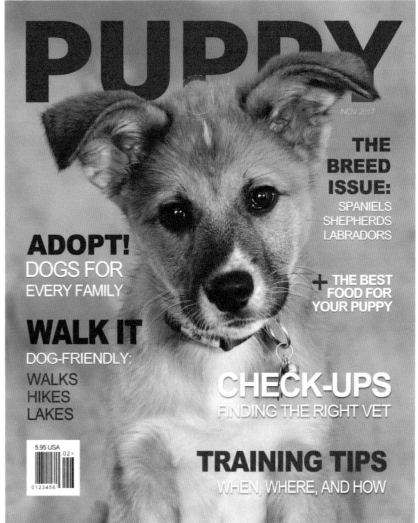

STEP 12

For this last step, I would like to refine the edge of my newly-created mask. First, I select the **Blur Mask** tool from the toolbar, set the **Amount** to **5**, and sweep across the top edge of the mask a few times.

Then I select the **Chisel Mask** tool, set the **Amount** to **1**, and brush over the top edge to chisel away a few pixels.

My magazine composite is now finished, so I save and close the file.

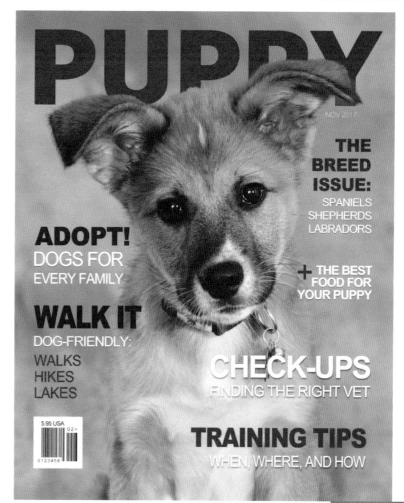

DOUBLE EXPOSURE

One of my favorite techniques to use in the Layers module is to create a double-exposure portrait. This effect can be accomplished with only a handful of layers and some blending modes, but creates dramatic results. For this photo, I will combine two photos, using the Develop, Layers, and Effects modules to create the final image.

STEP 1

I start in the *Browse* module and locate the *nicolesy-double-exposure-1.nef* file. I would like to do a quick edit to this Raw file before working on it further. So, I select this image and then click the **Develop** icon on the right to open it into the Develop module.

STEP 2

This image needs very little correction, but I would like to reduce the highlights on the face and bring out some of the shadow areas. I reduce the **Highlights** to **-24** and increase the **Shadows** to **17**.

In the *Color* section, I next increase the **Temperature** slider to **10** and reduce the **Tint** to **-15**. This helps to add some warmth to the skin tones.

When I'm finished, I click the **Browse** icon in the *Module Selector*, which closes the file.

STEP 1

STEP 2

135

STEP 3

In *Browse*, I locate the *nicolesy-double-exposure-2.nef* file, which will be the overlay for the double-exposure effect. I click on the image and then select the **Develop** icon in the *Module Selector* on the right.

STEP 4

The background of this flower is not pure white, so I will use the sliders in the Tone & Color section to help make the background closer to white. The flower is also in need of some additional brightness and color correction.

I start in the *Tone* section, where I increase the **Exposure** to **0.5**, the **Highlights** to **100**, and the **Whites** to **18**. This adds brightness to both the background and the flower.

Then, I increase the **Structure** to **24** to add some more detail to the edges of the flower.

I'm finished here, so I click the **Browse** icon in the *Module Selector* to close the file and go back to Browse.

STEP 3

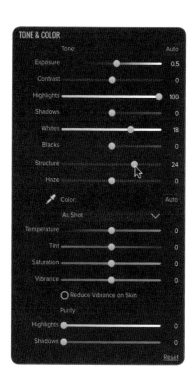

STEP 4

STEP 5

Now it's time to open both the portrait and flower files into ON1 Layers together. In the *Browse* module, I make sure that I can see both of these photos in the grid view by pressing the **G** key. I first select the *nicolesy-double-exposure-1.nef* file, and then I press and hold the **Cmd** (PC: **Ctrl**) key while clicking on the *nicolesy-double-exposure-2.nef* file. With these two images selected, I click the **Layers** icon in the *Module Selector*.

A window pops up asking "Do you want to add this photo as a layer, or open it as a new photo?" I select **Add as Layer**, and the images open into the Layers module, with each photo on its own layer.

To make things more organized, I rename the layers by double-clicking on each name in the Layers panel and typing names that make more sense: *Portrait* for the bottom layer and *Flower* for the top.

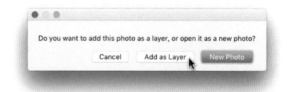

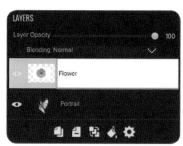

STEP 6

I'm going to begin working on the *Portrait* layer in order to hide some of the black background. First, I click the **eyeball** to the left of the *Flower* layer to hide that layer (for now) 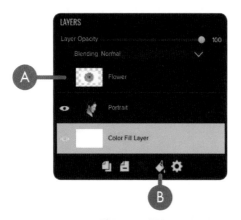.

Next, I click the **paint button icon** at the bottom of the *Layers* panel to add a **Color Fill Layer**. I choose **white** as the color, make sure that the **Blending Mode** is set to **Normal** and the **Opacity** is set to **100%**, and then I click **OK** to confirm those changes. Finally, I relocate this new layer to the bottom of the Layers panel.

STEP 7

Now it's time to start masking. I click on the *Portrait* layer in the Layers panel to activate it and select the **Masking Brush** from the toolbar. Then, in the options at the top, I make sure that the **Mode** is set to **Paint Out** and that the **Size** is set quite high (I have mine set to **500**). I also click on the **Perfect Brush** icon to activate it.

Then I sweep the brush over the area in front of the woman's face, careful to keep the center of the cursor only in the dark black areas. This creates a mask which hides the brushed areas and reveals the white color fill layer below.

STEP 7

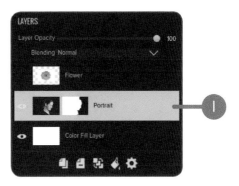

141

STEP 8

I need to refine the edges of the mask. First, I select the **Chisel Mask** tool from the toolbar, make sure that the **Amount** setting at the top is set to **1**, and then I sweep the brush over the front part of the image repeatedly until the dark edges have disappeared. For this image I am concerned with the masked skin areas only, so I ignore the hair for now.

STEP 9

The masked edge is quite harsh and jagged, so to help soften it I will use the **Blur Mask** tool. I select it from the toolbar, and at the top I set the **Amount** to **5**. I sweep once over the front portion of the image to soften the edge of the mask.

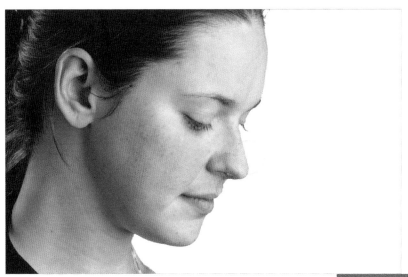

STEP 8

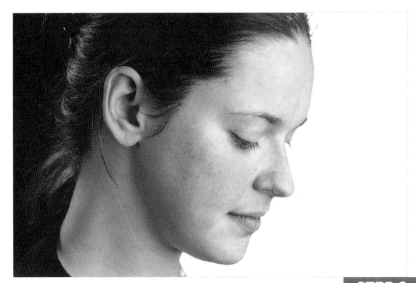

STEP 9

STEP 10

I'm done with the *Portrait* layer for now, so I move on to the *Flower* layer. I start by clicking once on the **Color Fill Layer** at the bottom, and then click the **Duplicate Layer** icon ⓙ. This creates a new duplicated layer of the white background. I then relocate this layer so that it is just below the *Flower* layer ⓚ, and I make the *Flower* layer visible again by clicking once on the eyeball to the left of the layer ⓛ.

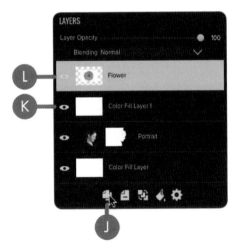

STEP 11

Next, I select the **Masking Brush** tool ⓜ and make sure that the **Mode** is set to **Paint Out**, the **Size** to **20**, and the **Feather** to **15** ⓝ. I zoom in and carefully brush along the bottom area of the image to mask away the stem from the flower.

I continue masking away all areas of this image around the flower until the background appears to be pure white.

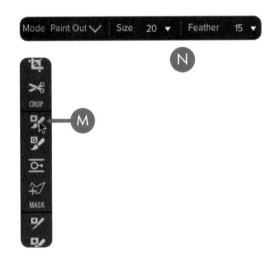

STEP 10

STEP 11

STEP 12

I would like this flower image to be combined with the white *Color Fill Layer* below, so with the top *Flower* layer active, I right-click over this layer and select **Merge Layers** . This merges the selected layer with the layer below it, so I now have one *Flower* layer with a complete white background .

STEP 13

Next, with the *Flower* layer still active, I click the **Blending** drop-down in the Layers panel and change the mode to **Screen**. This blends the flower with the portrait below.

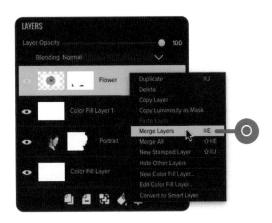

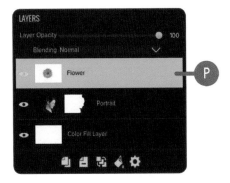

STEP 14

With the *Flower* layer still active, I activate the **Move** tool at the top of the toolbar. I zoom out to see more of the screen and then use my cursor to **rotate** and **resize** the flower until it is pleasingly positioned over the woman's face. I also am sure to put the center of the flower over her eye, which helps balance the image compositionally.

Once I have the *Flower* layer in position, I click **Apply** at the top of the screen to confirm my changes.

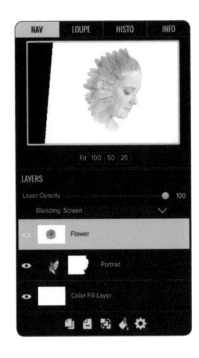

STEP 15

Next, in the *Layers* panel, I click on the *Portrait* layer to activate it. Then I select the **Masking Brush** from the toolbar, set the **Mode** to **Paint In**, and then roughly brush over the top part of the mask (near her forehead) to reveal more of the flower petals.

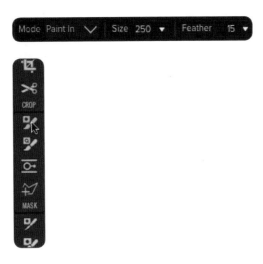

STEP 16

I need to refine this mask so that the petals look cleaner at the top near the forehead. I zoom in to see the area up close. Then, I set the Masking Brush **Mode** to **Paint Out** and change the brush's **Size** to **30**.

The areas I would like to mask are somewhat straight lines, so to mask this easily I start by clicking in one spot, holding the **Shift** key, and then clicking in another spot. This "draws" a line of brush stroke across this portion of the image.

Once I have the mask edge defined, I brush away the remaining portions of the unwanted petals.

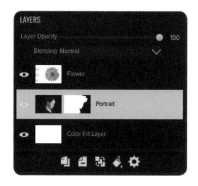

STEP 15

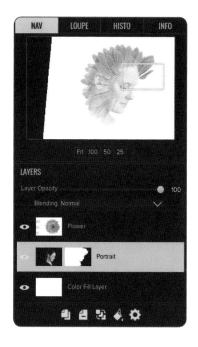

STEP 16

STEP 17

I am finished masking and creating this composite in Layers, but I would like to crop it so that it is a square. To do this, I select the **Crop** tool from the toolbar, and at the top I set the Ratio to **1x1 (Square)**. Then I position the crop so that the portrait is in the center of the frame.

STEP 18

I would like to bring this into Effects to apply a filter, but before I do that I need to combine the layers to create one flattened composite layer. To do this, I click on the top *Flower* layer. I right-click over the layer, and then select **New Stamped Layer**. This adds a new composite layer at the top of the Layers panel, but also keeps the original layers intact.

Before bringing the layer into Effects, I convert the layer to a *Smart Layer* by clicking the **gear icon** at the bottom of the Layers panel. This makes this layer re-editable.

STEP 17

STEP 19

With this Smart Layer active in the Layers panel, I click **Effects** on the right to bring the layer into the Effects module.

Once inside of *Effects*, I access the *Filters* tab on the left and select the **Split Tone** category. I scroll down until I locate the **Oats** filter, and click it to apply it to the image 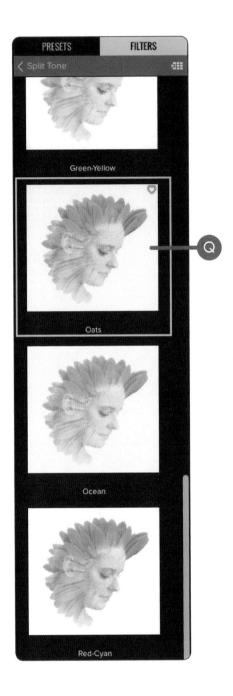. When I'm finished, I click the **Done** button in the bottom-right area of the window.

The image will open up into Layers, and if I look at the Layers panel, I will now see that there is an Effect applied to the top stamped layer ®. If I want, I can double-click over the Effects label to re-open the image into the Effects module to make further changes.

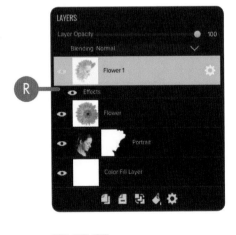

BEFORE

AFTER

CHAPTER FOUR

SPECIAL EFFECTS

ON1 Photo is not only a good tool to do basic processing, but it is also a great place to "level up" your photos by creating and applying special effects. Certain elements within the software, such as borders and textures, enable you to do this easily, and I will be demonstrating some of those features within this chapter. But there are many other ways to creatively edit a photo to get a different look, particularly by layering photographs or effects and combining them with blending modes and masking. In the following pages, I will show you how to create some enhanced photographs in both the Effects and Layers modules.

FOGGY LANDSCAPE

The right amount of fog can be a landscape photographer's best friend. It adds atmosphere, depth, and a moody quality to any photograph. The only problem is that fog is also quite unpredictable and not always easy to come by. In this tutorial, I will show you how to add a simple layer of fog over an image using a technique that can be applied to a wide variety of photographs as well.

STEP 1

I start in the *Browse* module where I select the *nicolesy-fog.dng* file. Then, I click the **Develop** icon in the module selector to open the photo into the Develop module.

STEP 2

The first thing I would like to do is crop the photo, as I feel this scene will be more compelling as a horizontal image. I click the **Crop** tool, and in the options at the top I select **Original Ratio** Ⓐ. Then I click the **Swap Width & Height** icon to switch the orientation of the image Ⓑ. When I have the photo properly positioned, I click **Apply** on the top-right of the screen.

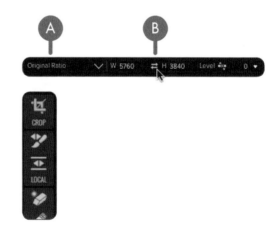

STEP 1

STEP 2

STEP 3

This photo is underexposed and in desperate need of tone adjustments. To get started I set the **Exposure** to **0.1** and the **Shadows** to **48**, which helps to reveal detail in the rocks.

Then, I set the **Haze** to **100** to add haze, which is the first step in creating the look of fog in the background.

Lastly, I increase the **Temperature** to **20** to add warmth to the image.

I'm finished with the photo here, so I will now move into Effects to start adding my fog effect. I do this by clicking the **Effects** icon in the *Module Selector*.

STEP 4

In Effects, I click the **Add Filter** button to apply my first filter and select **Glow** from the list. In the filter panel, I set the **Amount** to **55** and the **Halo** to **20**. Then, at the bottom, I change the **Mode** to **Screen**. This adds a soft white glow to the image.

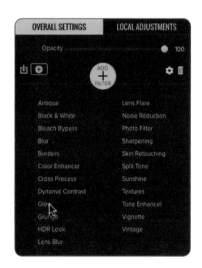

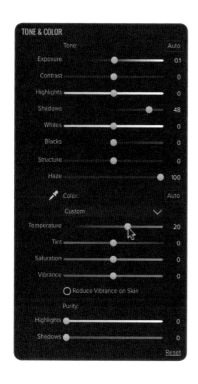

STEP 3

STEP 4

STEP 5

Next I click the **Add Filter** button and select the **Tone Enhancer** filter. This filter will be the main layer where I will add the fog effect.

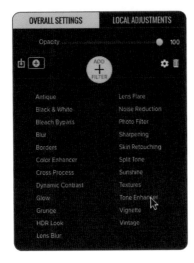

I start by reducing the **Detail** slider to **-10** to give the image a subtle blur. Then, I go to the bottom of this panel and click the **arrow** next to *Curves* to reveal the tone curve **C**. In the bottom-left quadrant, I click and drag on the point at the end of the curve line and drag up until the **Out** setting says **200** **D**.

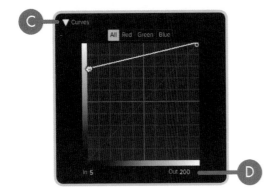

STEP 6

I don't want to apply this filter to the entire image, so I will create a series of masks on this one layer to blend the image and layer the foggy effect.

I begin by selecting the **Masking Bug** from the toolbar, making sure that the **Preset** in the options is set to **Linear Bottom**. Then, I click once on the bottom third of the image to apply the gradient to mask away the filter from the bottom of the frame.

Mask Preview:

STEP 5

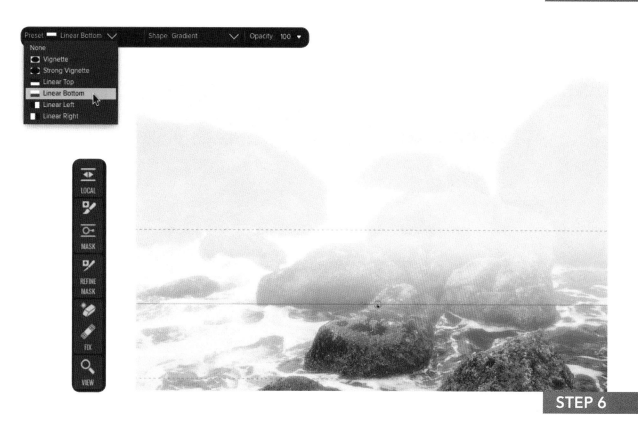

STEP 6

STEP 7

With the Masking Bug still active, I click the **Add** button on the top right to add another Masking Bug (graduated mask) with the **Linear Bottom** preset.

I **reposition** the bug so that it sits in the middle of the image, and then I click on the **dashed line** and extend it to increase the feather of this mask.

Then, in the options at the top, I reduce the **Opacity** of this mask to **50%**, which helps blend the center portion of the gradient in with the background.

Mask Preview:

STEP 8

I add one last mask by again clicking the **Add** button, and then make sure that the preset is also set to **Linear Bottom**.

I **reposition** this bug so that the center portion of the graduation is on the horizon line in the background.

Then, I set the **Opacity** of this mask to **25%** in order to reveal more of the fog effect in the middle areas of this graduated mask.

I now have three graduated masks applied to this filter to give the fog a "layered" look.

Mask Preview:

STEP 7

STEP 8

STEP 9

Now I would like to use the brush to mask out some more areas on the rocks. I select the **Masking Brush** from the toolbar, and at the top I set the brush's **Mode** to **Paint Out** and the **Opacity** to **20%**. I also activate the **Perfect Brush** with the keyboard shortcut **Cmd+R** (PC: **Ctrl+R**).

Next, I make two big sweeps: one over the cluster of "connected" rocks on the right and another on the large and small "connected" rocks on the left. I am careful to not lift up the cursor or stop and start brushing in the same area, because at this point I do not want to layer my brush strokes. (With a lowered brush opacity setting, the brush strokes will "add up" if you continue to lift up and brush over the same area again and again.)

After applying these first two strokes to get an even mask, I go back and brush over some of the rocks in the foreground because I want these rocks to have more detail and less fog than the rocks in the background.

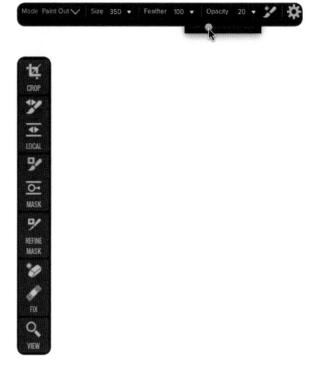

Mask Preview:

STEP 10

I'm finished adding the fog, and now I would like to add a bit of sharpening. I click **Add Filter** and select **Sharpening** from the list.

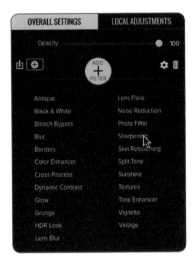

In the filter panel I choose the **Fix Focus** preset, but I would like to apply this to only the lower portion of the image. So, I select the **Masking Bug** from the toolbar, set the **Preset** at the top to **Linear Top**, and click somewhere in the lower half of the photo to apply the gradient mask.

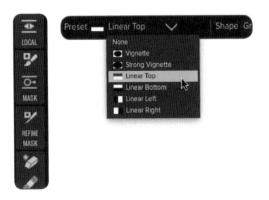

STEP 11

Next I would like to add one of my favorite filters, so I click **Add Filter** and choose the **Photo Filter** option.

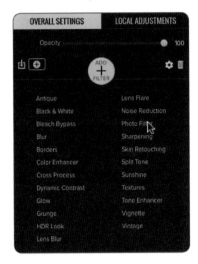

Then I use the **More** drop-down and select **Polarizer**. This adds a nice effect, but as in many of the previous steps, I would like to apply a mask. I click on the **Masking Bug** tool, set the **Preset** to **Linear Top**, and click on the top area of the image. This applies the polarizer effect to only the lower half of the photograph.

STEP 10

STEP 11

STEP 12

In the last step I would like to add a vignette. I click the **Add Filter** button again, and this time I choose the **Vignette** filter.

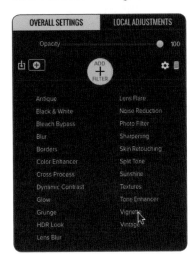

I select the **Big Softy** preset and increase the **Brightness** to **-84**.

Lastly, I click the **small square icon** at the bottom of this panel, which allows me to set the center of the vignette 🅔. I click on the rock that is in the lower-middle portion of the frame, and the vignette shifts slightly, making that area of the image the center.

That's it for this photograph, so I click the **Browse** icon to close my file.

BEFORE

AFTER

ANTIQUE PHOTO

ON1 Effects has quite a few filters and presets to help you age a modern-day photograph. You don't always need to rely one one-click presets to add this effect, however. In this tutorial I will show you how to take control of your edits and give a photograph an antique and old-fashioned appeal.

STEP 1

I begin by locating the *nicolesy-antique.dng* file in *Browse*, and then click the **Develop** icon in the *Module Selector*. This opens the file in the Develop module.

STEP 2

This image is well-exposed but could use a slight amount of adjustment. I click the **Auto** button at the top of the *Tone* section, which does a great job of adding a touch of brightness and contrast.

The color and white balance look good as-is, so I will leave those settings untouched.

Instead, I click the **Effects** icon in the module selector to go into Effects and add my antique stylization.

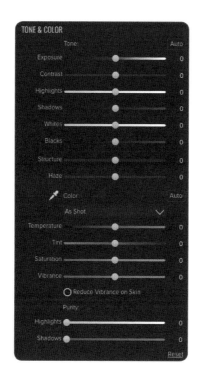

STEP 1

STEP 2

STEP 3

In Effects, I start by clicking the **Add Filter** button and selecting **Black & White**.

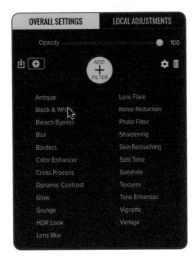

I select the **Red** filter, which adds a lot of punch and contrast to the tones. I don't want this photo to be black and white; I only want the tones to be affected. So, I click the **gear icon** at the top of the panel, and in the **Mode** drop-down I select **Luminosity**.

Then, to soften this filter's effect, I reduce the **Opacity** to **67%**.

STEP 4

I click the **Add Filter** button, and this time I select **Antique** from the list.

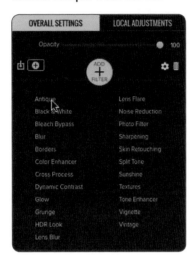

I select the **Warm** filter at the top of this panel, and then reduce the **Brightness** to **-13** to make the image a little bit darker. To soften the effect and reveal some of the image's original color, I reduce the filter layer's **Opacity** to **56%**

STEP 5

Next, I add another filter by clicking **Add Filter**, and then choosing the **Split Tone** effect. I like these default settings as-is, so I leave them alone and make no changes to this filter layer.

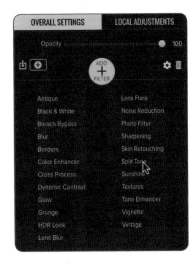

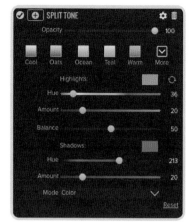

STEP 6

I photographed this image with a tilt-shift lens, so it already has a unique blur. I would like to intensify the blur, however, and add it to the edges of the photo. This will help give the image the look of being photographed with an old-fashioned lens. To add this blur, I click **Add Filter** and select **Lens Blur**.

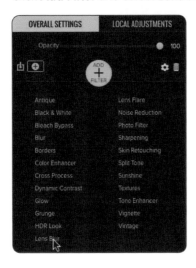

Then, in the filter settings, I increase the **Amount** to **34** and the **Quality** to **100**. I also reduce the **Brightness** to **-20** and the **Contrast** to **-100**.

This blurs the entire image, but I would like to have the blur affect only the outside edges. I click the **Masking Bug** in the toolbar, and in the options at the top I set the **Mode** to **Vignette**.

I then click once over the center of the image to add the mask and resize it with the **solid line** so that it is quite small.

Next, I drag the **dashed line** to extend the feather of the mask and soften the edge.

STEP 7

Now let's have some fun and add texture to this image. I click **Add Filter** and select **Textures** from the list.

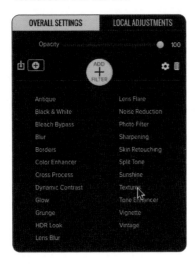

Next, in the **Category** drop-down, I select **Monochrome**. This first texture that is added, **Monochrome 01**, does a beautiful job of making the photo look like it has old and peeling emulsion.

To intensify the texture effect I set the **Mode** to **Normal**.

Next, I adjust the tone of the texture by reducing the **Opacity** to **47%** and the **Brightness** to **-19**. I also increase the **Scale** to **6**, which pushes the texture closer to the edges of the photo.

At the bottom of the panel, I click once on the **Flip Vertically** icon to flip the texture.

STEP 8

I click the **Add Filter** button and again choose the **Textures** filter. With this step I would like to add a camera frame to give the image the appearance of the photo being photographed with an older film camera.

I set the **Category** to **Photographic**, and in the texture drop-down I select **Ground Glass**. Then I reduce the **Brightness** to **-20** to darken the texture layer.

STEP 9

I would like to add some color and contrast "pop" to the image, so I add another filter by clicking the **Add Filter** button and select **Glow** from the list.

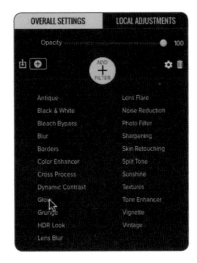

In the More drop-down I choose the **Charge More – Subtle** preset, and then reduce the **Opacity** slider to **60%** to soften the effect.

STEP 10

For this last step, I would like to give the photo a slightly matte look, so I click **Add More** and select **Blur** from the list.

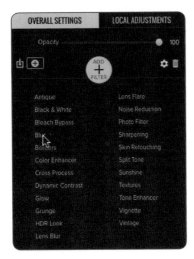

Then, I click on the **gear icon** at the top of this panel and change the **Mode** to **Exclusion**. This effect is quite intense, so I reduce the **Opacity** of this layer to **17%** to soften the effect and flatten some of the contrast in the image, giving it a proper vintage aesthetic.

BEFORE

AFTER

SEATTLE FIREWORKS

ON1 Photo has many features that allow you to create gorgeous composites. Although it may not be as robust as some layering applications, for photographers it has a very solid set of tools that can be manipulated to work in a wide variety of ways. In this tutorial, I will be placing photographs of fireworks onto a skyline image of Seattle, Washington and will be using very little masking. Instead, I will be taking advantage of the powerful set of blending modes included in the Layers panel. Let's get started!

STEP 1

I will start by doing some minor adjustments to the Seattle nighttime photo. I select the *nicolesy-seattle.dng* file from *Browse*, and then click **Develop** in the *Module Selector*. This opens the image into the Develop module.

STEP 2

In *Develop*, I begin by clicking the **Auto** button in the *Tone* section. This helps to boost the exposure and contrast, but the image could still use some brightness in the shadows. So, I increase the **Shadows** slider to **28**.

In the *Color* section, I reduce the **Temperature** slider to **-100** to remove some of the overwhelming warmth in the image and also increase the **Tint** to **8** to balance the colors in the image.

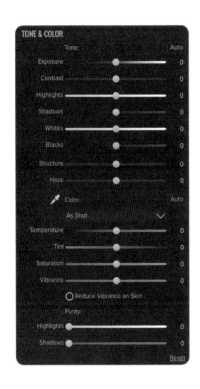

STEP 1

STEP 2

STEP 3

I notice that there are quite a few bright pixels and dust spots throughout the image that need to be removed. To do so, I select the **Retouch** brush from the toolbar, setting the **Size** to **20** and the **Opacity** to **100%**. Then, I zoom in to 100% and click over each spot to remove it. I also resize the brush as needed using the left and right bracket keys. I continue throughout the entire image until all spots are gone.

STEP 4

The photo looks a little crooked, so I select the **Crop** tool from the toolbar. Then, in the options at the top, I set the **Level** setting to **1** to make a subtle adjustment to the photo. When I'm finished, I click **Apply** in the top-right area of the window.

I'm finished with this photo, so I click **Browse** in the *Module Selector* to close the image.

STEP 3

STEP 4

STEP 5

Now I would like to do some minor adjustments to the fireworks images before adding them to the Seattle image. I start by selecting *nicolesy-fireworks-1.jpg*, and then click the **Develop** icon on the right.

STEP 6

Next, I would like to edit this photo so that the black areas are as pure black as I can make them. To do this quickly, I set the **Blacks** slider to **-100**. I decrease the **Contrast** to **-100** as well to bring back some of the subtle details along the outside edges of the fireworks.

When I'm finished, I click the **Browse** icon in the module selector to close this image and go back into the Browse module.

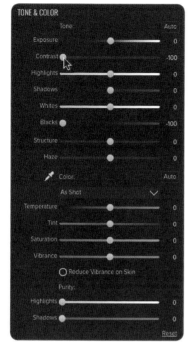

STEP 6

STEP 7

Now that I have the first fireworks image edited, I will sync those settings with the remaining photos.

I start by clicking on the *nicolesy-fireworks-1.jpg* file so that it has a blue border around it. I then right-click over the image and select **Copy Settings**.

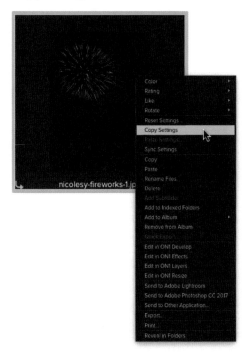

Next, I click on the *nicolesy-fireworks-2.jpg* file and hold the **Cmd** (PC: **Ctrl**) key while clicking over each of the other fireworks files one by one to select them. I right-click again over this group of images, but this time I select **Paste Settings**.

A window pops up asking which settings I would like to paste. I make sure that the **Develop** box is checked, and then click **Paste**. The Develop settings from the *nicolesy-fireworks-1.jpg* file are now copied over to the other fireworks images.

STEP 8

Now I would like to start blending these files together to create my composite. I begin by selecting the *nicolesy-seattle.dng* file and then clicking on **Layers** in the module selector to open this image as a PSD into the Layers module.

In the Layers panel, I rename this layer to *Seattle*. Next, I click the **Browse** icon in the *Module Selector* to go back to the Browse module to access the images of fireworks.

Note: The Seattle *document will remain open in Layers when I return to Browse.*

STEP 9

Back inside of *Browse*, I select all of the fireworks JPEG files, and then I click **Layers** on the right.

A window pops up asking me how I want to open these files. I click **Add as Layer** to add all four fireworks images to the opened *Seattle* document in the Layers module.

Once they are opened into Layers, I change each one's name in the Layers panel according to their filename (*Fireworks 1, Fireworks 2,* and so on).

STEP 8

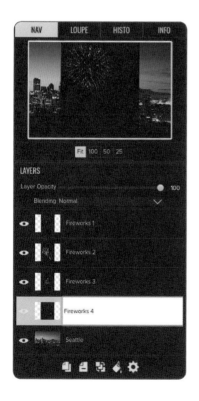

STEP 9

STEP 10

In the Layers panel, I hide the top three layers by clicking on the eyeballs to the left of the layer thumbnails so that only the *Seattle* and *Fireworks 4* layers are visible. With the *Fireworks 4* layer selected, I change its **Blending** mode to **Screen**, which hides all of the black sky in the photo surrounding the fireworks.

Next I select the **Transform** tool from the toolbar to resize, rotate, and relocate the *Fireworks 4* layer. When I am finished transforming, I click **Apply** at the top right of the screen to commit the change.

STEP 11

Now I will repeat this process with the next fireworks image. I select the *Fireworks 3* layer and click on the eyeball to the left of the thumbnail to reveal the layer. Then, I change **Blending** to **Screen** and use the **Transform** tool to resize, rotate, and relocate the layer so it is slightly overlapping a building on the right side of the photo. When I'm finished using the Transform tool, I click **Apply** to commit the change.

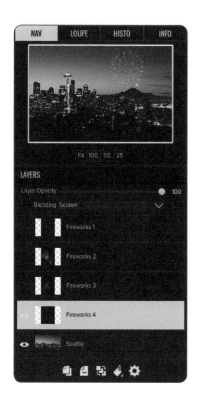

STEP 10

STEP 11

STEP 12

I would like to remove some of the fireworks lights, particularly the bright blob on the top of this layer, as well as the area where it overlaps the building. So I activate the **Brush** tool in the toolbar, and in the options at the top I set the **Mode** to **Paint Out**, the **Size** to **80**, and the Feather to **0**.

Next, I zoom in and mask away the overlapping area, along with the bright blob on the top-right portion of the fireworks.

STEP 13

I then highlight the next layer, *Fireworks 2*, make it visible by clicking on the eyeball to the left of the thumbnail, change **Blending** to **Screen**, and then use the **Transform** tool to resize, rotate, and reposition this layer.

Next I select the **Brush** tool, and with the options still in place from the previous step, I mask away some of the areas of the light trails that overlap with the buildings.

STEP 12

STEP 13

STEP 14

I highlight the very top layer, *Fireworks 4*, make the layer visible by clicking on the eyeball to the left of the thumbnail, and change the **Blending** mode to **Screen**.

Then, as I did with the previous fireworks layers, I activate the **Transform** tool and reposition and resize the layer over the Seattle skyline. When it is in place, I click the **Apply** button in the top right of the screen.

STEP 15

Next, I right-click on the top layer and select **New Stamped Layer**. This merges the layers below and puts the resulting composite on its own layer, while still keeping the original layers intact.

I set the **Blending** mode of this layer to **Soft Light** and reduce the layer's **Opacity** to **50%**. This intensifies the contrast and also adds a touch of saturation to the image.

STEP 14

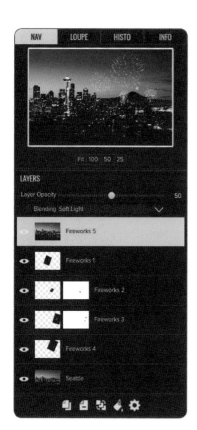

STEP 15

STEP 16

This new layer over-intensifies the shadow
areas in the lower half of the image, so I will
add a quick mask. I select the **Masking Bug**
from the toolbar, and in the options at the
top I set the **Preset** to **Linear Bottom**.

I then click in the center of the image to
apply this mask, which hides the bottom half
of the layer.

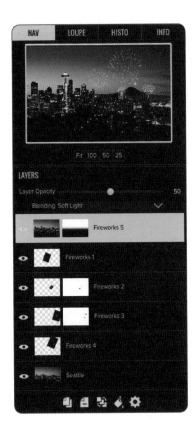

BEFORE

AFTER

CHAPTER FIVE

FINISHING TOUCHES

After you have created your masterpieces in ON1 Photo, there is still work to be done in order to get those photos out to the world. ON1 Photo can help you speed up some of the post-processing, and it offers several ways to export and display your images. This chapter is dedicated to prepping your final photographs to be proofed, printed, or posted on the Internet. Let's get to it!

BATCH-EDIT IN BROWSE

With this new version of ON1 Photo it is now incredibly easy to batch-apply presets to several photos at once. ON1 Photo RAW has the ability to save "global" presets, which include settings from both the Develop and the Effects modules. With this method you can take one photo from the same series, process it in both Develop and Effects, and then, in the Browse module, either copy and paste those settings or apply a saved preset from Presets panel in the left sidebar. Let's walk through this process with a group of images of my adorable nieces and nephews that I photographed in a pumpkin patch.

STEP 1

I will begin by opening one of my Raw photos into Develop: I highlight it, and then I click the **Develop** icon on the right.

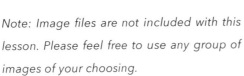

Note: Image files are not included with this lesson. Please feel free to use any group of images of your choosing.

STEP 2

In the Develop module, I make some basic adjustments to the *Tone* and *Color* sections, as well as add a subtle **Vignette**.

When I am finished, I click the **Effects** icon in the *Module Selector* to open the image into the Effects module.

STEP 1

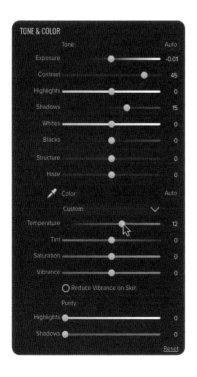

STEP 2

STEP 3

Now, inside of *Effects*, I would like to apply some filters to add some stylization to this. I will start by clicking **Add Filter**, and then I choose **Sunshine** from the list.

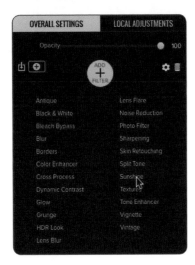

In the filter panel, I click the **Natural** preset and reduce the **Opacity** to **75%**.

STEP 4

Next I will convert this to black and white, so I click **Add Filter** and then choose the **Black & White** filter from the list.

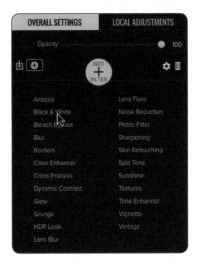

In the filter panel, I choose the **Red** preset, which adds a nice contrast to the black-and-white conversion.

STEP 3

STEP 4

STEP 5

I click **Add Filter** once again, and this time I choose **Glow** from the list.

Then, I click the **More** drop-down and select the **Rich Glow** preset. This adds a nice soft effect to the portrait.

STEP 6

I want this photo, along with the other images from this series, to be previewed as they might look if printed with a white matte. To do this, I click **Add Filter** and then select the **Borders** filter.

The default border for this filter, the **White Square** border in the **Simple** category, is exactly what I need. I keep this border in place, and in the settings near the bottom, I increase the **Fit Image** slider to **8** to reveal more of the original photograph inside of the border.

STEP 5

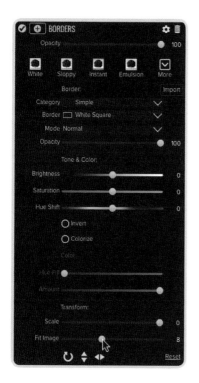

STEP 6

215

STEP 7

I'm finished processing this image, but because I plan on applying these settings to other photos, I first need to save a preset.

I click the **Save Preset** icon in the *Overall Settings* section, type in a name for the preset, make sure that both the **Develop** and **Effects** boxes are checked, and then click **OK**. This creates a preset that I can now apply to other photographs.

Note: You can also save a preset by going to the menu and selecting **Settings > Save Settings as Preset**.

STEP 8

Next, I click the **Browse** icon to go back into Browse. I press the **G** key to make sure that I am in grid view, and use the keyboard shortcut **Cmd+A** (PC: **Ctrl+A**) to select all of the photos in the folder.

In the left sidebar, I click the **Presets** tab at the top and navigate to my saved preset. With all of the images still highlighted, I click the preset I just created and ON1 batch-applies it to the selected photos.

STEP 8

STEP 9

The beauty of this process is that you can try out many different presets on a large batch of photos very quickly. For example, let's say that I also want to see what these same photos look like with another preset applied.

In the *Presets* panel, I navigate to the **Faded & Matte** category. With all of the images still selected in Grid view, I click on the **Faded Matte - Cool** preset. After a few moments the selected photos now have a different preset applied.

This is a great way to create large batches of stylized images, which can be good for proofing or exporting to show a client.

■ ■ ■

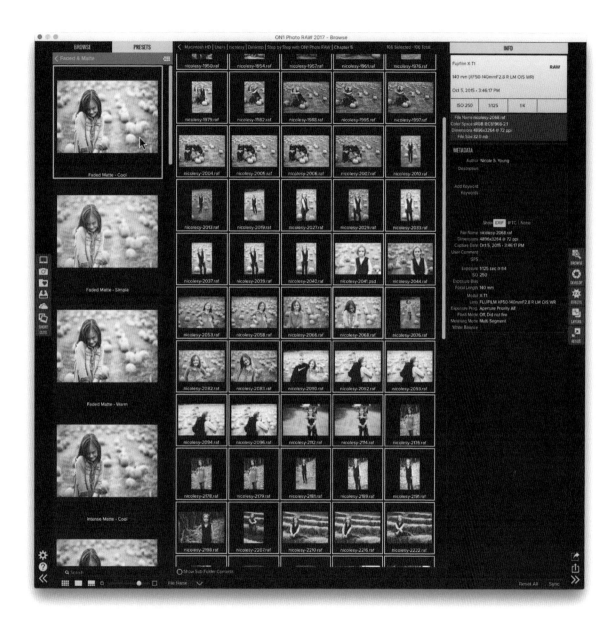

EXPORT A DIGITAL COPY

Most often the last step in my photography workflow, especially if I don't intend on printing a photo right away, is to share the image online. ON1 Photo makes it easy to quickly export a photo or a group of photos from either the Browse, Develop, or Effects modules. In this tutorial, I will walk through the steps to export a photo from the Browse module so that it is the proper file size and resolution to share online.

STEP 1

I begin in the *Browse* module, and I locate a file I would like to export. (I want to export only one photo, but I could also select a group of images and export them all at the same time.) Then, I click the **Export** icon in the bottom-right area of the application. (You can also choose **File > Export** in the menu to access the Export panel.)

After I click the icon, a new panel appears on the right side of the application. This is the *Export* panel, and it is where I choose the settings I will use to export the image.

Note: An image file is not included with this lesson. Please feel free to use any of your own images to follow along.

STEP 2

There are three open panels in this default view. I will start out with the top panel, *File Type*. First, I set the top drop-down to **JPEG** and make sure that the **Quality** slider is at **100%**. This will ensure that my file is displayed at the best quality possible when I share it online.

Next, I set the **Color Profile** at the bottom of this panel to **sRGB**, which is the ideal color space for most web browsers.

STEP 3

In the next panel, *Location*, I select where I want this image to be saved by choosing **Folder**. I then click the **Choose** button and navigate to my desktop. This will make It easy to locate the file once it has been exported.

I also ensure that **Prevent Overwrite** is selected so that if I already have a file with the same name in that location it will not automatically replace that file.

Then, in **After Export**, I choose the **Show In Finder** option. Setting this will automatically open the folder where this image is saved after the export.

STEP 4

In the *Filename* panel, I click the **plus icon** next to the *Current Name* setting at the top, then I use the drop-down to select **Text**.

Next, I type some additional text that I would like to add to my filename. Because I will be sharing this on my blog, I type "-blog" so that it will be added to the end of the original filename after export.

STEP 5

I would like to resize this image as it is exported so I am not posting the full-resolution file online. This will speed up the image loading in the web browser, and it is also a small precaution to help prevent copyright infringement.

To access the *Photo Size* panel, I go to the top of the Export sidebar and click the **plus icon** next to the *Export/Resize* text. Then I choose **Photo Size** from the list, and a new panel appears below.

In the panel, I set the **Resize to** option to **Long Edge** and type **2000** in the box below. This will resize the image so that it is no more than 2000 pixels tall or wide, depending on the image's orientation. I also set the **Resolution** to **72**.

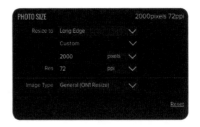

STEP 6

I'm finished with the export settings, but because this is a common export type for me, I will first save it as a preset.

To do this, I will click the **Preset** drop-down at the top and select **Save New Preset with Current Settings**.

A window pops up, so I give my new preset a name and click **Create**. Later I can access this preset for other images and quickly apply all of these settings.

STEP 7

It's time to export the photo! I click the **Export** button on the bottom-right area of the window, and the photo is exported to my desktop. Now I can upload this photo to my blog to display it online.

thailand-8163-blog.jpg
2,000 × 1,333

TILE A PRINT WITH RESIZE

Here I have a beautiful scene I photographed in Iceland and merged as a panorama using Adobe Lightroom. I would love to print this, but would like to first break it up into three equal-sized square tiles before sending it to a specialty printer. To do this, I will use the Resize module, an excellent place to prepare a photograph to be printed.

STEP 1

I start by locating the *iceland-pano.psd* file in Browse, and then I click the **Resize** icon at the bottom of the *Module Selector*. This opens the image into the Resize module.

Note: When working on filetypes that are not PSD, this process will convert the image into a flattened PSD copy.

STEP 2

Now I will go into the panels on the right to make some adjusments before tiling the photo. I will not be enlarging this image, so I skip the *Document Size* and *Settings* panels and focus on the *Sharpening* Panel. I make sure that this panel has a **blue check mark** to make it active.

STEP 2

STEP 3

Whenever I sharpen a photo, I always make sure that I am zoomed in close. I do this because I don't want to oversharpen the image; I need to make sure I can see the changes up close when moving the sliders and settings.

I set the **Zoom** to **100%** and scroll to an area with both mountain and sky in my preview. Now as I make adjustments in the Sharpening panel, I can easily see those changes take place.

With the **Type** set to **Unsharp Mask**, I increase the **Amount** to **70**. Then, in the *Protect* section at the bottom of this panel, I increase the **Highlights** slider to **100** to prevent the panel from sharpening too much of the bright sky.

STEP 4

Now I'm ready to start tiling my panorama. First, I set the **Zoom** to **Fit** so that I can see the entire image in the preview area. Next, I click in the circle to the left of the *Tiling* panel to make it active.

I want to tile this photo into three tiles from left to right, so I first set the **Width** drop-down to **Columns** and the Height drop-downs to **Rows**. Next, I set the **Width** to **3** and the **Height** to **1**.

STEP 5

When I look at the *Output* dimensions in the Tiling panel, the **Tile Size** says it is **7.02 x 7.31 inches**, which is not perfectly square. I need to crop the overall image to make the width and height of each tile equal.

I select the **Crop** tool from the toolbar on the left, and then turn my attention to the options at the top of the window. I want the **Height** to be exactly **7.02 inches**, so I click and drag on the top of the crop box and move it down until it reads **7.02 inches**. When I have it set properly, I click **Apply** in the top-right section of the window.

Now when I look in the Tiling panel, the Tile Size is set to a perfect square (7.02 x 7.02 inches).

Note: If you are unable to get it to the exact measurements, try moving the crop box as close as you can, clicking Apply, and manually typing the dimensions into the Height box.

STEP 4

STEP 5

STEP 6

I'm ready to export these tiles so that I can send them off to be printed. I set the **File Type** to **JPEG** and click the **Choose** button. Here I create a new folder on my desktop so that the images are easy to locate after they are rendered.

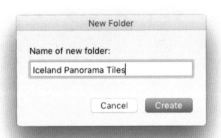

Next, I click the **Done** button on the bottom of the window, and the files are exported to the folder I selected. Now I can upload these three square images to have them printed, and when I arrange them side by side I will have my complete panorama photo.

I uploaded the panorama files to Bumblejax.com and had them printed on metallic paper, framed inside of acrylic blocks.

C O N C L U S I O N

Photography is a very important part of my life, and the work that happens after the images are created can be just as crucial to the process as setting up the camera and pressing the shutter. I not only write and teach about this software, but I do in fact use it regularly with my own photographs, and I have found ON1 Photo to be an excellent tool in polishing and adding that extra *je ne sais quoi* to my images.

There are so many possibilities for processing, styling, masking, layering, and blending in ON1 Photo. What you have found in this book is just the tip of the iceberg. My hope is that you will take the techniques learned throughout these lessons and creatively apply them to your own photographs. Or, better yet, that you will experiment and discover your own unique uses for the tools within this software.

Nicole S. Young

INDEX

O

P

T

Temperature
   double exposure, 134-135
   foggy landscape, 160-161
   landscapes, 90-91
   lionfish, 52-53
   magazine cover effect, 122-123
   portrait, 70-71, 76-79
   Seattle fireworks, 190-191
   sky replacement, 102-105
text, adding to filenames, 222
texture effect, intensifying, 182-183
textures, importing, 33
Textures filter, adding for antique photo, 184-185
Thumbnail size, Browse workspace, 16-17
tiles, splitting images into, 39
Tiling panel Resize workspace, 42-43
tiling prints with Resize, 224-231
Tint slider
   lionfish, 52-53
   magazine cover effect, 122-123
   portrait, 70-71
   Seattle fireworks, 190-191
   sky replacement, 102-105, 114-115
Toggle left section (open/close)
   Browse workspace, 16-17
   Develop workspace, 22-23
   Effects workspace, 28-29
   Layers workspace, 34-35
   Resize workspace, 40
Toggle right section (open/close)
   Browse workspace, 18-19
   Develop workspace, 24-25
   Effects workspace, 30-31
   Layers workspace, 36-37
   Resize workspace, 42-43
Tonal Contrast, sky replacement, 114-115
tone, correcting for magazine cover effect, 120-121. See also
   Split Tone effect
Tone & Color
   black-and-white conversion, 64-65
   Develop workspace, 24-25
tone curve, revealing for foggy landscape, 162-163

Tone Enhancer
   foggy landscape, 162-163
   sky replacement, 114-115
Tool Options bar
   Develop workspace, 22-25
   Effects workspace, 28-31
   Layers workspace, 34-37
   Resize workspace, 40, 42-43
Transform tool
   Layers workspace, 34-35
   magazine cover effect, 126-127
   Seattle fireworks, 200-205
Trim tool in Layers workspace, 34-35
tulips. See landscapes
Type drop-down, landscapes, 96-97

U

underwater images, 52
Unsharp Mask, using to tile prints with Resize, 226-227

V

Vibrance slider, adjusting for portrait, 76-77
Vignette
   antique photo, 180-181
   batch-editing Browse, 210-211
   foggy landscape, 170-171
   landscapes, 96-97
   lionfish, 60-61
   portrait, 86-87
   sky replacement, 118-119
Vignetted preset, black-and-white conversion, 66-67

W

Warm filter, adding for antique photo, 176-177
warmth, removing from Seattle fireworks, 190-191
white balance
   landscapes, 90-91

Z

www.nicolesy.com

Made in the USA
Lexington, KY
09 July 2017